The Convict Christ

The Convict Christ

What the Gospel Says about Criminal Justice

✠✠✠

Jens Soering

ORBIS BOOKS

Maryknoll, New York 10545

Founded in 1970, Orbis Books endeavors to publish works that enlighten the mind, nourish the spirit, and challenge the conscience. The publishing arm of the Maryknoll Fathers and Brothers, Orbis seeks to explore the global dimensions of the Christian faith and mission, to invite dialogue with diverse cultures and religious traditions, and to serve the cause of reconciliation and peace. The books published reflect the views of their authors and do not represent the official position of the Maryknoll Society. To learn more about Maryknoll and Orbis Books, please visit our website at www.maryknoll.org.

No part of this publication may be reproduced or transmitted in any form or by any means, electronic or mechanical, including photocopying, recording, or any information storage or retrieval system, without prior permission in writing from the publisher.

Queries regarding rights and permissions should be addressed to:
Orbis Books, P.O. Box 308, Maryknoll, NY 10545-0308.

Manufactured in the United States of America.

A version of the Introduction was published in *PRISM* (Evangelicals for Social Action), March–April 2005. A version of chapter 6 was published in *The American Conservative,* September 27, 2004, and in *The Hook,* October 14, 2004. A version of chapter 7 was published in *Celebration,* October 2004. A version of chapter 8 was published in the *Washington City Paper,* September 3–9, 2004. A version of chapter 13 was published in *America,* December 6, 2004. Portions of chapter 14 were published in the *National Catholic Reporter,* March 19, 2004; *This Rock,* February 2003; *Pastoral Life,* March 2003; and *Emmanuel,* May–June 2003.

Library of Congress Cataloging-in-Publication Data

Soering, Jens.
    The convict Christ : what the Gospel says about criminal justice / Jens Soering.
      p. cm.
    ISBN-13: 978-1-57075-648-1 (pbk.)
    1. Imprisonment – Religious aspects – Christianity. 2. Punishment – Religious aspects – Christianity. 3. Criminal justice, Administration of. 4. Christianity and justice. I. Title.
HV8687.S66 2006
261.8′336 – dc22

                                    2005028512

To Bernd, Dick, and Sarah,
my guardian angels,

and Calvin, Kevin, Richard, and Sam,
in memoriam

On Good Friday, 1957, Karl Barth spoke at a church service conducted within the walls of a prison in Basel, Switzerland:

Here they hang all three, Jesus and the criminals, one at the right and one at the left, all three exposed to the same public abuse, to the same interminable pain, to the same slow and irrevocable death throes.

These two companions were evidently and undeniably criminals, evil people, godless people, unjust people. And [Christ], like them, was condemned and sacrificed as a lawbreaker, a criminal. All three were under the same verdict.

This was the first Christian fellowship, the first certain, indissoluble and indestructible Christian community. Christian community is manifest wherever there is a group of people close to Jesus who are with him in such a way that they are directly and unambiguously affected by his promise.

Consider this fact: Jesus died precisely for these two criminals who were crucified on his right and on his left and went to their death with him. He did not die . . . for the pious, but for the godless, not for the just, but for the unjust. . . .

We are such people, all of us — you in this house which is called a prison — [and] those of us outside who have different experiences yet are, believe me, in the same predicament. In reality we *all* are these people, these crucified criminals. And only one thing matters now: are we ready to be told what we are? Are we ready to hear the promise given to the condemned?

— Karl Barth, *Deliverance to the Captives**

*London: SCM Press, 1961, 76, 81, 77, 81, 83.

.

Contents

Foreword

J ENS SOERING writes to us from his prison cell about his personal
faith experiences and his love for Jesus, whom he describes as
"the convict Christ." Jens tells us the stories of inmates through the
lens of the scriptures. He reflects on today's criminal justice system
from a Gospel perspective.

I found *The Convict Christ* both fascinating and enriching. It
provides food for thought on scripture passages that are all too
familiar and not fully appreciated. The author provides multiple examples, quotations, statistics, and analyses of the so-called criminal
justice system, which is decidedly bankrupt.

The author confronts the everyday realities of prison life from
the Gospel message of mercy, compassion, and forgiveness. It is
shocking to realize that Jesus was condemned to death as a common
criminal, with two criminals on crosses next to him. Jesus revealed
the self-sacrificial nature of divine love.

An added feature at the end of each chapter are questions for
reflection and discussion.

I recommend *The Convict Christ* for those willing to become
more deeply sensitized to the failures and injustices in our jails and
prisons today.

WALTER F. SULLIVAN
Bishop Emeritus of Richmond
Former President of Pax Christi USA

Acknowledgments

S PECIAL THANKS go to my research elves: Dick Busch, Lewise Busch, Mary Edwards, Sarah Gallogly, Tom Keating, and Stan Lloyd; my technical support team, Wayne Carter and Meredith Sweet; and, as always, my "midwife" Ann Rainey. I could not even have attempted this book without their active help and encouragement. Any mistakes of fact or errors in tone are, of course, entirely my responsibility, not theirs.

Introduction

✠✠✠

WHEN GOD CHOSE to take on human flesh, he did not become a priest or a monk, a king or a general, a poet or a philosopher. Instead, he became a death row prisoner, a condemned criminal executed alongside two thieves. Nothing else would do: the living image of the invisible deity could take no truer form than a "dead man walking," the lowest of the low.

Yet we somehow manage to overlook this central fact of our faith. When we think of Jesus, we prefer the beautiful baby in Mary's arms, the miracle worker, the eloquent preacher, or the resurrected Son sitting on a cloud next to his Father. Christ is indeed all of those — but he *saved* us by submitting himself to capital punishment as a convicted felon. His most important work was to die as a common criminal.

To say that Jesus was not a "real" convict because he did not commit any crime is to miss the point entirely, of course. Since the mid-1990s, more than 140 prisoners in this country have been exonerated through DNA tests, and every one of them was a "real" convict before being proved innocent. A convict is merely a person who has been tried, sentenced, and (in capital cases) executed, *regardless* of his or her actual guilt. Thus Joseph the Israelite was a "real" convict, even though he did not actually rape Potiphar's wife — and so was our Messiah (Genesis 39:7–20).

And, indeed, having his Son classed as a felon was part of God's plan, as Christ explained at the Last Supper: "It is written, 'And he was numbered with the transgressors'; and I tell you that this must be fulfilled in me. Yes, what is written about me is reaching its fulfillment" (Luke 22:37; Isaiah 53:12).

1

Moreover, becoming a convict was not merely a role that Jesus assumed like a divine play-actor. In the parable of the sheep and the goats, he said explicitly, "I was in prison and you came to visit me.... Whatever you did for one of the least of these brothers of mine, you did for me" (Matthew 25:36, 40). Just as Christ became a full, true human being at birth, he became a full, true jailbird at death.

So scandalous is this fact that even our major Bible translations subtly obscure it. Luke 23:32, for instance, is often rendered, "Two other men, both criminals, were also led out with him to be executed," implying a difference between the two thieves and Jesus. But the original Greek text of this verse reads *de kai heteroi kakouroi duo sun auto:* the two other criminals also with him. Thus the evangelist Luke recognized an equivalence between Christ and the thieves that is apparently considered too shocking by modern translators.

For the earliest Christians, however, becoming a prisoner was nothing to be ashamed of. "Whoever serves me must follow me," their master told them, so virtually all of the apostles did time behind bars and were eventually executed by the state — just like Jesus (John 12:26). And in the Roman amphitheaters, thousands of first- and second-century believers died as criminals, members of an illegal revolutionary movement.

Perhaps those early followers of the Way accepted a convict's death so readily because they had a deeper insight into the full meaning of the cross than we do today. Of course all Christians then and now understand that, through the crucifixion, Christ revealed to us the self-sacrificial nature of divine love: "For God so loved the world that he gave his one and only son" (John 3:16). Or, as the beloved disciple put it, "This is how we know what love is: Jesus Christ laid down his life for us. And we ought to lay down our lives for our brothers" (1 John 3:16). However, the cross also illustrates perfectly the human sin for which the Son of God died in expiation.

At the Last Supper, he told his disciples that "this is to fulfill what is written in their Law: 'They hated me without reason' " (John 15:25; Psalm 35:19, 69:4). Christ was referring to persecution by the world: his imminent trial, conviction, sentencing, and execution (John 15:20, 18). Because "they have hated...me," Jesus' opponents deliberately put him to death as part of a judicial proceeding and thus stand "guilty of sin [and] have no excuse for their sin" (John 15:22).

So perhaps we can complete the apostle John's thought in his above-quoted letter by saying, "This is how we know what sin is: hating Jesus Christ enough to execute him. And we ought to refrain from doing the same to our brothers."

That is a daring and provocative restatement of the meaning of the cross, of course. To see Christ's self-sacrificial death as the ultimate expression of love is comfortable and familiar — though not especially challenging, since none of us really expect to have to give our own lives for our brothers. But to see Jesus' execution as the sum and substance of evil is strange and unsettling, since it calls into question our own criminal justice system. For how can we justify using police and court procedures today that are virtually identical to those used to prosecute Christ two thousand years ago?

In our own, supposedly more civilized age, the authorities still hire undercover informants — just like Judas. Tactical squads still go out at night to make arrests — just like the soldiers at Gethsemane. And under certain circumstances, interrogators still slap suspects around to obtain confessions — just like the Sanhedrin.

All of us still enjoy a nice, spectacular, high-profile trial — just like the crowd outside Pilate's palace. Judges are still sometimes swayed by public opinion to find defendants guilty despite their own doubts — just like Pilate. Appeals courts still tend to uphold a trial court's verdict even when there are procedural errors — just like Herod, who refused to overturn Pilate's decision.

Unfortunately, some prison guards still humiliate and abuse convicts — just like the soldiers who had charge of Jesus. And in some cases, we still cheer when the death penalty is imposed on an especially heinous criminal — just like the rabble at Golgotha.

Are we supposed to believe it was *wrong* to do all this to Jesus, but *right* to do it to the two thieves, "one on his right, the other on his left" (Luke 23:33)? Or is it possible that our Father wants to teach us, through the cross, that we should not do such things to *any* of his children?

To answer that question, we will examine what Christ himself had to say about criminal justice, a subject he raised with surprising frequency in the Gospels:

- At the very beginning of his public ministry, immediately after his temptation in the desert by the devil, Jesus went to the synagogue in Nazareth and laid out a detailed campaign platform for his mission: "to preach good news to the poor, ... *to proclaim freedom for the prisoners* and recovery of sight for the blind, [and] to release the oppressed" (Luke 4:18, emphasis added).

- "Freedom for the prisoners" apparently referred not only to metaphorical prisoners of sin, but to a literal convict doing time for assault: the Gerasene demoniac, who "had often been chained hand and foot" but was now freed by Christ from the improvised lock-up in the town cemetery (Mark 5:4; see also Matthew 8:28).

- When confronted with an ordinary criminal found guilty of a capital offense — the woman caught in adultery — God's Son did not hesitate to intervene and released her from death row (John 8:1–11).

- Despite the considerable risk of retaliation by King Herod, our Lord held a public speech of support for his cousin, John the Baptist, who had been thrown in jail for criticizing this corrupt ruler (Matthew 11:2–19).

- Mark's description of John the Baptist's execution at King Herod's banquet does not mention Christ directly, but this incident illustrates well the utter callousness with which prisoners' lives are often treated (Mark 6:17–29).

- In the parable of the good Samaritan, Jesus reminds us that we need to listen to the cries of anonymous, possibly unsympathetic crime victims in the ditch even when we are busily rushing along the road of life on important business of our own (Luke 10:29–37).

+ The parable of the persistent widow features another power-less person crying for help — and, to us perhaps surprisingly, an "unjust judge" who refuses her pleas (Luke 18:6).

+ In the parable of the sheep and the goats mentioned earlier, Christ explicitly threatens us with the "eternal fire prepared for the devil" if we fail to recognize *his* face in the faces of "the least of these brothers of mine...in prison" (Matthew 25:41, 40, 36).

+ Perhaps most significantly, our Lord described the Holy Spirit as a defense lawyer (*parakleitos* in Greek, *advocatus* in Latin) who protects us in court from an accuser or adversary (*satanos* in Greek) (John 14:15ff., 15:26–16:16; Matthew 10:20).

+ Before Jesus' execution, the young Roman soldiers in the Praeto-rium "stripped him" and "mocked him" and "struck him" and "spit on him," much as the young American soldiers tormented Iraqi prisoners at Abu Ghraib in our own age (Matthew 27:28, 31; Mark 15:19).

+ As the legionnaires led Christ toward Golgotha, the man they chose for the degrading task of carrying the cross just happened to be Simon of Cyrene — Cyrene being a town on the northern coast of Africa whose residents were probably darker in skin tone than ordinary Jerusalemites (Mark 15:21).

+ During his final moments on earth, knowing he was about to die, our Savior did not utter a few last words of wisdom to his disciples or cure one last leper, but instead ministered to the two common criminals on the crosses next to his — and succeeded in saving one (Luke 23:38–43).

+ The so-called "bad thief" whom Jesus could not save is often ignored by Christians who prefer to focus on the "good thief's" more inspiring example; but despair is a sad reality of every pris-oner's life, and its bitter fruit was displayed right next to Christ at the very end.

+ Of the three convicted felons executed on Golgotha, one rose from the grave and thereby saved me, another prisoner, from dying physically and spiritually two thousand years later (see Philippians 3:10–11).

Thus both our Lord's death and his resurrection are the most eloquent answer to our earlier question, whether the cross is meant to tell us something specific about sin and criminal justice. God's Son died as a criminal, and the *very first* person whom he raised to new life and took "with me [to] paradise" was a thief (Luke 23:43). Just a coincidence?

To help us explore that question with greater specificity, we will meet some real, live jailbirds in these pages — actual criminals whose lives illustrate what a Gerasene demoniac, for instance, might look like in our own age. These convicts' stories will help us examine on a direct, practical level what Christ's example can teach us about the treatment of prison inmates today. When it comes to crooks and criminals, what would Jesus do?

And how are *we* living the Easter message — the message of the convict Christ?

A Note from the Author

Some readers of this book may see my description of Jesus as a prisoner as self-serving, since I have been continuously incarcerated since 1986. To this charge I plead guilty. Christ did "not come to call the righteous, but sinners," so I believe he has a special interest in lowlifes like me and "had to be made like [me] in *every* way" to redeem me (Mark 2:17; Hebrews 2:17). I selfishly claim Jesus as my older brother and Savior.

Questions for Reflection and Discussion

1. Jesus Christ had to lay down his life for us to save us from our sins. Can you think of any other ways — besides being executed as a criminal — that he might have accomplished this divine purpose? For instance, could Jesus have given his life as a soldier in battle? Or could he have allowed himself to die of leprosy? How would a different kind of death have shaped our faith?

2. This introduction points out parallels between the legal process by which Christ was put to death and the methods employed by modern law enforcement, court and correctional officials. Can you think of more parallels? Examples: the via dolorosa and the "perp walk," the sign on the cross above Jesus' head and Internet registries of criminals, the taunting of the crowd at Golgotha and the TV program *Cops*.

3. Carefully examine your own emotional reaction to this book's premise, that Christ died a convict's death. Do you recoil from this idea? Does it embarrass you — and why? Are you surprised that you never noticed this central element of the Passion narrative before? Why do you think you did not see this until now?

ONE

The Sermon in the Synagogue at Nazareth

America's Prison Crisis

✠✠✠

I MAGINE a modern-day politician announcing his candidacy with a speech like the following:

> Vote for me, and I will not help the rich, nor will I give tax breaks to the middle class. Instead, I will help the poor: the convenience store clerks earning minimum wage, the cleaning crews who work in the skyscrapers at night, and the unemployed who find no room in homeless shelters.
>
> Vote for me, and I will not hire any more police officers, nor will I toughen any laws. Instead, I will release no less than half of all prisoners currently serving time in jails and penitentiaries across this nation. America is supposed to be "the land of the free," but we have the highest incarceration rate of any country in the world. Let's change that: Free the felons!
>
> Vote for me, and I will not make sure that your HMO rates stop rising every year, nor will I require insurance companies to supply free Viagra through their prescription plans. Instead, I will furnish decent, nuts-and-bolts health care to all those tens of millions of Americans who have no medical coverage at all right now.

> Vote for me, and I will grant American citizenship to all
> illegal immigrants, the invisible millions who do our society's
> dirty work for a pittance but cannot even send their children
> to our schools or get a driver's license. Their oppression has
> lasted long enough; let's welcome them into our family!

Of course we all know what would happen to a political candidate
who made such promises today. So it is all the more surprising that
Christ held a speech not too different from the imaginary one above
at the very beginning of his public ministry two millennia ago.

Immediately after his baptism by John and his forty-day prayer
retreat in the desert, "Jesus returned to Galilee in the power of
the Spirit" and went to the town synagogue, the center of politico-
religious power in his time and country (Luke 4:14). There he
announced the four central planks of his campaign platform for
bringing in the kingdom of heaven:

> The Spirit of the Lord is on me,
>   because he has anointed me
>   to preach good news to the poor.
> He has sent me to proclaim freedom for the prisoners
>   and recovery of sight for the blind,
>   to release the oppressed,
>   to proclaim the year of the Lord's favor.
>   (Luke 4:18–19)

And then, almost in passing, the Bible notes the most astonishing
part of this incident in Christ's life: "*All spoke well of him* and were
amazed at the gracious words that came from his lips" (Luke 4:22,
emphasis added). What a difference two thousand years make! Instead of dismissing Jesus as a political dreamer or condemning him
as a dangerous radical, the people of Galilee *praised* him for wanting to help the needy, the incarcerated, the physically handicapped,
and the disenfranchised.

Why do American Christians today look askance at the same four
policy initiatives that the Palestinian Jews of Christ's era applauded?
When I raise this question, I am often told that it is premised on a
misinterpretation of scripture: Jesus' speech in that synagogue was

not meant to address the *social* problems of poverty, penal reform, health care, and discrimination at all. He was concerned with the poor *in spirit,* the prisoners *of sin,* the *spiritually* blind, and those oppressed *by demons* — so I am told.

But my Bible makes clear that this spiritualized interpretation of our Messiah's mission cannot be the whole truth:

- Christ fed the hungry crowds literal bread and fish (Matthew 15:32);
- He saved a real death row convict from execution by stoning (John 8:1–11);
- Jesus restored literal eyesight to blind Bartimaeus (Matthew 10:46–49);
- He spoke at great length with a real Samaritan woman, whose gender and second-class national heritage made her doubly oppressed (John 4:1–16).

Of course our Lord released all four of these men and women from the bonds of sin and guilt. But since Christ is God incarnate, the invisible Spirit taking on human flesh, the liberation he brings must also go beyond the spiritual to the physical. So it truly is puzzling that we close our eyes precisely to those marginalized people whom Jesus freed from hunger, capital punishment, chronic illness, and the stigma of social exclusion.

Many Christian churches do, of course, take up our Lord's challenge and operate soup kitchens, offer hospice care to indigent AIDS patients, and work with Salvadorean refugees. Even in such socially active faith communities, however, prisoners are frequently neglected in favor of more obviously deserving recipients of charity. Yet Jesus ranked prisoners *second* in his campaign platform, *ahead* of the blind and the oppressed.

This peculiar blindness toward penal issues extends beyond religious circles to the general population of America. As I write these lines during Lent of 2004, this country cages a greater percentage of its own citizenry than any other nation on earth. More than China, more than North Korea, more than Iran — more than anyone! Nearly one-quarter of all prison inmates on the entire planet are housed in U.S. jails and penitentiaries, even though less than 5 percent of the world's population is American.[1] Yet no one in this country thinks this worthy of comment.

Not even liberals seem concerned that the U.S. incarceration rate *septupled* between 1973 and 2003, from just under 100 inmates per 100,000 civilians to just over 715 per 100,000.[2] While progressives protested against apartheid in the 1980s and 1990s, when South Africa locked up 851 black men out of 100,000, they quietly accept that their own government imprisons 4,834 African American males out of 100,000.[3] But gay marriage rights and the near-extinction of the three-toed Alaskan ringworm — *those* are declared to be national priorities by the left.

Nor are U.S. conservatives any less blind in this regard. Always quick to debunk Democratic boondoggles, the Republicans stayed silent as Departments of Correction became the largest and most expensive government agencies in many states, costing this nation a total of $57 billion per year.[4] Even more surprising is that the right failed to note how ineffective all those expensive new jails and penitentiaries were in terms of public safety: the domestic crime rate in 2003 was *exactly the same* as in 1973.[5] The same results, at seven times the price — and not a single howl of conservative protest!

What the United States cannot or will not see, other countries certainly can and do: "The American incarceration rate is . . . the highest in the world, but it has not made the United States a safer place to live," the Correctional Service of Canada noted recently.[6] Our northern neighbor locks up only 116 felons per 100,000 compared to our 715, yet its crime victimization rate is virtually identical to America's.[7]

In fact, *all* industrialized nations, *including* the United States, have nearly the same crime victimization rates, ranging in a narrow band between 21 and 24 percent of the total population.[8] But those other "first world" countries manage to achieve this level of public safety with incarceration rates of just 50 to 125 per 100,000 — with some, like Germany (at 96 per 100,000), actively seeking to *lower* their rates.[9] That is why, "among mainstream politicians and commentators in Western Europe, . . . the criminal justice system of the United States is an inexplicable deformity [that] arouses incredulity and incomprehension," according to Baroness Vivian Stern, an internationally recognized penologist and member of England's House of Lords.[10]

So I ask again: why do neither American Christians nor secularists see prisons and prisoners as urgent problems, while both the Galilean Jews of Jesus' age and other industrialized nations today do?

Perhaps the answer lies in history and national identity. Both the residents of the Roman province of Palestine and the citizens of Western European countries had and have direct, recent experience of being conquered by foreign armies and thus becoming prisoners in their own lands. In Europe, only England was never militarily occupied in the twentieth century — and, not surprisingly, that nation has Europe's highest incarceration rate, at 125 per 100,000. (Spain, too, was never invaded, but experienced an especially brutal civil war from 1936 to 1939; most Irishmen saw the English as occupiers until the declaration of the Irish Free State in 1922; and while Switzerland and Sweden were never physically occupied by the German *Wehrmacht,* they lost virtually all independence during World War II.)

In the case of the Jews who praised Christ's inaugural speech, with its promise of "freedom for the prisoners," their whole identity as a people was founded on their two past captivities in Egypt and Babylon and, of course, their current subjection to Roman rule. Not only that, but some of Israel's founders and national heroes were actual prison inmates:

- Joseph the Israelite, who later saved the lives of his entire family, was thrown "into the jail where the royal prisoners were confined" after Potiphar's wife accused him of rape (Genesis 39:40);

- Israel's great early champion and defender Samson "was put to grinding in the prison" of the Philistines after his betrayal by Delilah (Judges 16:21);

- Jeremiah, the last of the major prophets, was thrown "into the cistern of Prince Malchiah, which was in the quarter of the guards" and served as Jerusalem's jail (Jeremiah 38:6).

As Jesus and his later audience in that synagogue were growing up, they undoubtedly played at being Samson, breaking out of jail, and smiting even more Philistines hip and thigh with the jawbone of an ass! An astonishing thought for Americans, perhaps, since neither George Washington nor Thomas Jefferson did time behind bars — but those *jailbirds* were *role-models* for Christ and his contemporaries. And that personal identification with the plight of convicts may explain why the Jews of two thousand years ago, unlike modern-day Christians in this country, accepted the liberation of prisoners as a sensible, even laudable proposal by an up-and-coming leader like Jesus the carpenter's son.

This Jewish sympathy for convicts and outlaws extended to the first generation of Christians, as scripture tells us clearly even if we lack ears to hear. Of course we all remember what Paul wrote the church at Corinth:

> Not many of you were wise by human standards; not many were influential; not many were of noble birth. But God chose the foolish things of the world to shame the wise; ... he chose the lowly things of this world and the despised things — and the things that are not — to nullify the things that are, so that no one may boast before him. (1 Corinthians 1:26–29)

Most of us even realize that "the lowly things of the world" must have included a great number of slaves, since Paul and Peter repeatedly included special sections with advice just for them in their epistles: 1 Corinthians 7:21–24; Ephesians 6:5–9; 1 Timothy 6:1–2; 1 Peter 2:18–25. Slaves were a kind of prisoner too, of course, but in fact the earliest Christian communities included a number of actual felons — and how many of us noticed *that,* given our blindness to prisoners?

No, I do not mean the apostles themselves, though virtually all of them were executed as common criminals by the Roman authorities. Here I mean the rank-and-file believers who filled the pews on Sundays, according to Paul:

> Neither the sexually immoral nor idolaters nor adulterers nor male prostitutes nor homosexual offenders nor *thieves* nor the

greedy nor drunkards nor slanderers nor *swindlers* will inherit the kingdom of God. *And that is what some of you were.* (1 Corinthians 6:9–11, emphasis added)

In fact, some of those "thieves" and "swindlers" had not yet given up their illegal handiwork entirely, as Paul implies elsewhere: "He who has been stealing must steal no longer, but must work" (Ephesians 4:28). And in the only personal letter of Paul's to be included in the New Testament, he offers to repay Philemon anything that his escaped slave Onesimus had stolen from him: "If he has done you any wrong or owed you anything, charge it to me. I, Paul, am writing this with my own hand — I will pay it back" (Philemon, vv. 18–19).

When Paul wrote his letter to Philemon during his pretrial confinement in Rome, he had already done time in many jails across the Near East, often "praying and singing hymns to God [for] the other prisoners" (Acts 16:25). So he had first-hand experience of what Joseph and Samson and Jeremiah had suffered, and he must have had strong personal feelings about Jesus' call for "freedom for the prisoners" so many decades earlier. In our age and in this country, we have lost touch with this theme of our faith — and that is much to be regretted.

Of course those 2.2 million men, women, and juveniles currently incarcerated in the United States regret our neglect of prisons and prisoners.[11] But those of us not serving time behind bars, as Paul and Peter and John did, have lost something as well: a sense of what "that old-time religion" really meant in those days when our faith was young and fresh and growing. What a thrill it must have been for the apostles to seek out "the foolish…, the lowly…, the despised," and to recognize Christ's image in *their* faces — even if those faces belonged to convicts! If American Christians could recapture just a little of that spirit today, their own lives might be filled with the same kind of power and excitement that Paul experienced as he prayed and sang with his fellow jailbirds.

And if "freedom for the prisoners" were not just proclaimed but promulgated today, this nation's shamefully high incarceration rate could perhaps be lowered to the same level as that of other civilized countries. Then America could one day call itself "the land of the free" again — maybe.

Questions for Reflection and Discussion

1. Try to imagine how America might see its history differently, and perhaps would have become a different sort of country, if the British Army had captured George Washington and Thomas Jefferson early on in the Revolutionary War, put them in prison for several years, and released them only after the colonies won independence.

2. How did the fact that President Nelson Mandela spent twenty-seven years in prison shape the first few years of South Africa's history after the ending of apartheid?

3. Were you surprised by some of the statistics about America's modern-day love affair with prisons, cited in this chapter? Why do you think you have not heard until now that septupling the U.S. incarceration rate has not lowered the crime rate at all? *Cui bono?*

4. As someone who pays taxes and thus financially supports this country's enormous correctional departments, do you think you bear any personal responsibility for this state of affairs? If yes, how urgent do you consider this problem — if you consider it a problem at all? Will this issue affect your vote in the next election?

TWO

The Gerasene Demoniac

Mental Illness behind Bars

✣✚✣

I N CHAPTER 1 we noted that Jesus Christ, as God incarnate, could not offer us freedom from our spiritual afflictions only, but also had to address this-worldly problems like physical hunger, literal incarceration, real chronic illness, and actual social exclusion. Our specific area of interest in this book is prisoners, of course, and a quick search of the Gospels soon provides us with an example of Christ freeing a bona fide jailbird from the hoosegow. The episode occurs fairly early in Jesus' travels as a preacher, when he goes to the Gerasene territory and heals the demoniac.

"Though he was chained hand and foot and kept under guard," this dangerous criminal "had broken his chains and [now] lived in the tombs outside town," in lieu of prison (Luke 8:29, 27). Not only was he "so violent that no one could pass that way," but he also "had not worn clothes" in quite a while (Matthew 8:28; Luke 8:27). "Night and day among the tombs and in the hills he would cry out and cut himself with stones," the Bible tells us, so he must have been bloody as well as naked and unkempt (Mark 5:5). A frightening and no doubt disgusting sight.

Yet Christ healed him, "dressed" him in whatever extra clothes the disciples had brought with them, and even gave him a job: "to tell in the Decapolis how much Jesus had done for him" (Luke 8:35; Mark 5:20). An amazing thought: the first apostle to the gentiles was not St. Paul, after all, but this nameless ex-convict from the region of the Gerasenes.

That is all very touching and inspiring, of course, but hardly relevant to our own age. Nowadays, people like the Gerasene demoniac are housed in secure mental hospitals for the criminally insane, where they are given psychotropic medication and therapy to help them, yet are confined to keep the rest of us safe. So we do not need Christ's assistance anymore, at least not with the likes of the Gerasene demoniac — right?

Wrong.

Of America's 2.2 million prison inmates, at least 20 percent — over 400,000 — are *officially certified* as mentally ill by correctional medical departments.[1] And those are only the ones we know about: the true number is actually much higher, since 40 percent of jails and 17 percent of state penitentiaries do not even bother to evaluate the psychiatric status of their prisoners.[2] By contrast, only 80,000 patients are still housed in secure mental wards today,[3] thanks to the massive closures of forensic psychiatric hospitals around the country in the 1970s and 1980s.

Thus "prisons have really become, in many ways, the de facto mental hospitals," according to former correctional psychologist Thomas Fagan, Ph.D.[4] But prisons, unlike hospitals, do not provide psychiatric services to their inmate patients: Iowa's correctional department, for instance, has only three psychiatrists for more than eight thousand prisoners, while Wyoming's state penitentiary has a single psychiatrist on duty — for two days each month.[5] As a result of this lack of treatment, mentally ill inmates frequently stay in their prison's punishment blocks for years on end, according to a recent study of New York's Department of Correctional Services. Fully 25 percent of the inmates in that state's punitive segregation units are diagnosed as mentally ill, and half of those surveyed attempt to commit suicide while confined there.[6]

So what do the Gerasene demoniacs of our own age look like?

They look like Oliver T., for example. In 1979, Oliver was convicted of armed robbery and aggravated assault and sentenced to more than sixty years behind bars. Sometime in the 1980s, he began to call himself Olivia instead of Oliver — a not-uncommon phenomenon among inmates who are forced into sexual servitude by older, stronger prisoners. I met him in 2004, in his twenty-third and my eighteenth year of incarceration.

By this time, Oliver had taken to carrying a little purse on his wrist as he pranced around the penitentiary. No one objected, until one of the guards told him he could not take it into the kitchen, where he worked. Feeling insulted and challenged in his femininity, Oliver/Olivia became disruptive and had to be frogmarched to the punishment block to cool his high heels for a while.

Oh, yes, all very funny — a bit disgusting, of course, but not without humor. There goes that crazy Olivia again, the girl's gone wild! How the rest of us convicts laughed. . . .

That night in the punishment block, Oliver cut open his scrotum with an old razor blade in an attempt to castrate himself. Then, according to a staff member I trust, he wrote in blood on the wall, "I am a woman."

"Night and day among the tombs and in the hills he would cry out and cut himself with stones" (Mark 5:5).

After returning from the hospital, where the doctors reattached what they could, Oliver was placed in the prison's infirmary, and I was called to his bedside. I was the facility's "inmate advisor": when convicts are "written up" for breaking a rule, "inmate advisors" assist them in their defense at the subsequent disciplinary hearing. Oliver had received a "charge" for violating "Category II Offense Code 234 — Self-mutilation or Other Intentionally Inflicted Self-injury," and I had to be present during the service of the disciplinary offense report to ensure that his due process rights were not violated.

Because I was trusted — relatively speaking — by the guards here, they usually let me serve the paperwork myself. I entered the infirmary room and found Oliver lying on his side on a bed, with a guard sitting directly across from him to prevent him from injuring himself again. Standing next to the bed, I read out the gruesome disciplinary offense report without getting any reaction from Oliver at all; he appeared to be dozing.

Then I began to read the questions at the bottom of the offense report — do you want witnesses at your hearing? do you wish to attend the hearing? that sort of thing — the first one of which is, "Yes/No — Request inmate or staff advisor." Again Oliver gave no response, no sign he even heard me. Proper procedure at this stage is to read the question three times and then write in the space provided, "Refused to respond." After doing so now, I added a question not printed on the form, one I do not usually ask while serving a charge: "Oliver, do you want my help?"

Oliver raised his head, looked directly into my eyes, and said, "Yes."

That "yes" is the reason I am telling you his story. I was not able to help Oliver in any other way, so this is all I can do for him. I cannot say "no" to his "yes"; I will not.

Oliver refused to respond to any other questions. Later that day, he was moved back to the punishment block and strapped down in a special cell equipped for that purpose, using what is called "five-point restraint." There are over four hundred thousand Gerasene demoniacs behind bars, remember, so by now suitable accommodations have been prepared for them in every prison.

The state in which Oliver and I are serving time has a small psychiatric prison for completely uncontrollable inmates — a natural next stop for him, one would have thought. But for some reason that facility refused to accept Oliver, and so he was sent to another prison with a special housing unit for mentally ill convicts. Unfortunately, that type of unit does not provide much in the way of therapy beyond a daily dose of strong sedative pills. And after residents have been "stabilized" there, they are moved back into normal housing units with regular convicts.

And the cycle of being abused, and acting out, and getting strapped down begins all over again.

There is no happy end to this story, unfortunately. In fact, we have a new self-mutilator in this prison's punishment block right now: an eighteen-year-old kid nicknamed "Cut Me Up," who, at stressful times, begins to imagine there is cancer beneath his skin that he must cut out himself, because no one else cares. Well, he is right about one thing: no one else cares.

Certainly the guards do not care what happens to "Cut Me Up" when they put him in a cell with an "old head," a long-term prisoner like me. To many a convict who has not seen a woman in twenty or thirty years, a fresh young thing like "Cut Me Up" is a dream come true, nearly as good as making parole. What happens next is stressful enough to make anyone think about cutting up his arms and chest.

During a hearing before the U.S. Congress on the Prison Rape Reduction Act in July 2002 a former state attorney general testified that "anywhere from 250,000 to 600,000" inmates were forced to have sex against their will each year.[7] The result is an HIV infection rate of at least 8.5 percent in New York state's correctional system, which tests its prison population more rigorously than others. By comparison, the estimated infection rate for the civilian U.S. population is 0.3 percent.[8]

So, twenty-four years from now, when "Cut Me Up" is roughly the same age that Oliver/Olivia is now, we can expect him to leave some red writing of his own on the wall of some punishment block somewhere. His message, like Oliver/Olivia's, is not hard to read; it is, in fact, the same as that left on King Belshazzar's palace wall in Daniel's days: *"Mene, Tekel and Peres. . . . You have been weighed on the scales and found wanting"* (Daniel 5:25, 27). To which the prophet added elsewhere: "Therefore, O King, take my advice: atone for your sins by good deeds, and for your misdeeds by kindness to the poor" (Daniel 4:24).

If those instructions are not clear enough for our times and our criminal justice context here, King Solomon gives us a tutorial in what we are supposed to do with Oliver/Olivia and "Cut Me Up":

> Rescue those being dragged away to death,
>> and from those tottering to execution, withdraw not.
> If I say, "I know not this man!"
>> does not he who tests hearts perceive it?
> He who guards your life knows it,
>> And he will repay each one according to his deeds.
>> (Proverbs 24:11–12)

"Remember those in prison as if you were their fellow prisoners, and those who are mistreated as if you yourselves were suffering," the author of the letter to the Hebrews wrote hundreds of years later, but in the same spirit (Hebrews 13:3). The times may change, but the message on the wall does not.

No doubt it was precisely in *this* spirit that Jesus got into his boat and took that long trip to the home of the demoniac. Christ did not care what crimes this man had or had not committed, nor did he wait to begin his prison ministry until he had nothing better to do. And he did not turn back even when a squall blew up en route and threatened his boat. Jesus cared.

Of course he knew whom he would meet as soon as he reached the other side of the lake: Oliver/Olivia and "Cut Me Up." Lunatics and criminals, "chained hand and foot" in five-point restraints, "being dragged away to death" in a punishment block (Luke 8:29; Proverbs 24:11). In Christ's eyes, they were worth the time, trouble, and danger. Are they worth it in yours?

If your answer is yes, and if you *act* on that answer, then perhaps this story has the beginnings of a happy end after all.

Questions for Reflection and Discussion

1. As Jesus crossed Lake Galilee to visit the Gerasene demoniac, a storm blew up that threatened to sink his boat (Luke 8:22–24). Do you expect to face similar difficulties — the sudden emergence of personal problems, the disapproval of friends — if you begin to engage in prison ministry or penal reform activities? What can you do to prepare yourself for such opposition?

2. As a matter of social policy and law, do you think that it really matters where mentally ill men and women are housed — in large psychiatric hospitals as before, or in prisons as today?

3. Did you know that, according to the congressional testimony cited in this chapter and U.S. Department of Justice statistics, there are actually more *men* raped in America every year (250,000 to 600,000) than *women* (89,000 to 141,000)?[9] Why do you think you have not heard of this until now?

4. Both the Gerasene demoniac and Oliver/Olivia are obviously offensive, even repulsive in any number of ways. How would you feel if you were to meet, say, a schizophrenic who has committed a serious assault and now smears himself with feces in a prison's punishment block? Would you be scared? Disgusted? Overwhelmed?

THREE

The Woman Caught in Adultery

The Death Penalty

✠✠✠

J ACK C. is a stone-cold killer. When he was seventeen years old,
he took one of his father's semi-automatic pistols, illegally converted it to fully automatic, and used it to kill a college student
whom he barely knew. Jack did not simply shoot this innocent
young man: he emptied the gun's entire clip into his body. As a
back-up, "just in case," he had carried a revolver with him, so there
can be no doubt about his murderous intentions.

Jack was tried as an adult because he committed this crime in
the mid-1990s, when school shootings topped the news. Strangely
enough, the judge failed to sentence him to the maximum — life in
prison — and imposed a term of only fifty-six years. So Jack will
get to walk free again one of these days, unlike that college student
whose life he took so prematurely.

That is one way to tell the story of Jack C. and the murder he
committed. But it is not the only way. Just for a few minutes, let us
look at this crime from a different perspective.

Jack's father was an engineer whose work required him to move
to a different city on an annual basis. Because he took his family
with him, his son never had the opportunity to settle down: every-
where he was the new kid in town, and every year there was a new
town. Unfortunately, Jack was also quite small — five feet five and
110 pounds — as well as loudmouthed. So he was frequently teased
and taunted and bullied as he was growing up.

24

Jack's primary escape from the ridicule of his ever-changing classmates was to go hunting with his father. Deep in the silent woods, there was no one to pick on him, and he and his father could share their love of guns. Collecting firearms became a way for them to bond, so Jack's father naturally trusted his son to handle their weapons responsibly.

Back in school, however, the bullying grew worse and worse — until one day Jack could take no more. He rushed home, retrieved the two guns described earlier, and then sprayed half a dozen bullets at the first person on whom he could unload all his pent-up frustration and anger. In fact, the college student whom Jack killed was not even an especially egregious bully, but just the older brother of one of his primary persecutors.

After using his pistol to murder this innocent young man, Jack shot himself in the head with the revolver he had also carried along. But he only blew away part of his jaw, a lot of teeth and half of his tongue. Many operations later, you have to look twice before you notice all the scars underneath his chin. And of course he lisps a little, with only half a tongue.

Jack will be released in 2044, when he will be sixty-five years old. Thanks to the "truth in sentencing" reforms enacted in the 1990s, he has to serve between forty-eight and fifty-one years of his fifty-six-year sentence. There is absolutely no way he can get out any earlier; there is no more parole, no more time off for good behavior, and certainly no governor's clemency for the likes of Jack.

This is, of course, a death sentence on the installment plan. After five decades in prison, Jack will have no contacts at all in the community to which he returns and very little idea of how to handle life on the outside by himself. Presumably he will freeze to death under a bridge somewhere shortly after gaining his "freedom."

To the family and friends of Jack's victim, that may seem like justice at long last. No amount of teasing and taunting could excuse what he did to their son, brother, and friend. "An eye for an eye," the Good Book says; the ultimate crime deserves the ultimate punishment.

Of course it is not my intent here to attempt to justify his crime. But hearing *all* of Jack's story, including "his" side, offers those of us who are not directly affected by this homicide an opportunity to reflect on what Jesus would do if he were confronted with Jack today. In fact, he already met Jack once — roughly two thousand years ago, when the scribes and Pharisees brought a woman caught in adultery to him for judgment (John 8:1–11).

By our standards, marital infidelity is a private moral failure, not a capital crime like Jack's murder, so executing an adulteress strikes us as absurd. But to understand what Christ did on this occasion, we must keep in mind the standards of *his* time and culture. And in Palestine in AD 33, breaking one's marriage vows was indeed a crime so grave that it deserved the death penalty (Leviticus 20:10).

Jesus explicitly accepted this Pentateuchal law, as all the others — "I have not come to abolish them but to fulfill them" — and he did not attempt to defend the woman on the grounds that her crime was somehow less serious than, say, murder (Matthew 5:17). Instead, Christ challenged the authority of her judges to carry out the stoning: "If any one of you is without sin, let him be the first to throw a stone at her" (John 8:7). Thus it is overly simplistic and unscriptural to portray our Messiah as an outright opponent of capital punishment.

When given the opportunity to affirm the death penalty directly and openly, however, the Son of God refused. Strange.

Even stranger, Jesus' Father also refused the option of execution when confronted with the very first crime of any kind in biblical history, Cain's murder of Abel (Genesis 4:1–16). Like Jack C., Cain too had spilled human blood for base motives. Yet Yahweh did not make an example of Cain to deter future criminals, but merely sentenced him to banishment (Genesis 4:12–13). And when Cain complained that even this was too harsh, God reduced his punishment still further by giving him special protection (Genesis 4:15).

Strange indeed. Especially since Yahweh explicitly included murder as one of the many crimes that merited the death penalty (Exodus 21:12–14).

What could explain the Father's and the Son's reluctance to impose the ultimate punishment prescribed by their own divine law? The prophet Ezekiel explains:

> But if a wicked man turns away from all the sins he has com-
> mitted, if he keeps all my statutes and does what is right and
> just, he will surely live, he shall not die. None of the crimes he
> has committed shall be remembered against him.... As surely
> as I live, says the Lord God, I swear I take no pleasure in
> the death of the wicked man, but rather in the wicked man's
> conversion, that he may live. Turn, turn from your evil ways!
> (Ezekiel 18:21–22, 33:11)

"Turn, turn from your evil ways" — this pronouncement of Yahweh's sounds very similar to what Christ told the adulterous woman:
"Go now and leave your life of sin behind" (John 8:11).

Interestingly enough, however, God no more condemned the
death penalty outright in this passage from Ezekiel than Jesus did
in the Gospel of John.

Perhaps we can reconcile this split by recalling the original purpose of capital punishment, which was not *judicial* (as in our age)
but *religious*. "The land can have no atonement for the blood shed
on it except through the blood of him who shed it. Do not defile
the land," Moses taught the Israelites on Mount Tabor (Numbers
35:33). Because murder was a stain on the entire community that
lived on "the land," it was necessary to "purge from your midst the
guilt of innocent blood" in order to restore Israel's relations with
Yahweh (Deuteronomy 21:9).[1] This ritual purification and cleans-
ing of the entire people was represented symbolically by carrying
out the execution "outside the camp" and by requiring "the whole
community" to participate in the stoning of the offender (Numbers
15:36).[2] In fact, if a particular homicide went unsolved, the priests
were required to execute a heifer in place of the actual murderer
(Deuteronomy 21:8).

The primarily religious function of capital punishment in pre-
Christian Israel meant, however, that relatively few offenders were
in fact executed. According to modern scriptural scholars, "The
laws of all societies contain ideal norms that are not actually
enforced in life. This appears to be the case in a considerable
number of biblical laws, whose ideal and *reforming* character is
patent."[3] And since there is not much "reforming" or "turning

from evil ways" that can be done after stoning, the Pharisees of Jesus' time were "not apt to be harsh in their punishments," Josephus tells us in his *Antiquities* (XIII:294) (Ezekiel 33:11). Indeed, sentencing just one person to death in seven years earned a court the label "destructive," according to the Mishnah tractate *Sanhedrin*.[4]

Even before Jesus appeared on the scene, then, stoning was no longer Israel's preferred means of "purg[ing] from your midst" the guilt of violating Yahweh's laws (Deuteronomy 21:9). And after Christ's death on the cross, capital punishment finally lost any remaining expiatory purpose: our Savior "offered for all time one sacrifice for sins" (Hebrews 10:12). Whereas once the land could "have no atonement...except for the blood" of the offender, "we have now received reconciliation [or: atonement]...through the death of [God's] Son" (Numbers 35:33; Romans 5:11, 10).

Thus when the thief on the cross next to Jesus said, "We are punished justly, for we are getting what our deeds deserve," Christ did not contradict him because, indeed, "the wages of sin is death," and the Mosaic code provided for execution (Luke 21:41; Romans 6:23). However, even as the thief was correctly affirming the justice of the death penalty, the Son of God was paying those wages for him and for us. "By *his* wounds you are healed," and by Jesus' wounds — not his own — the thief, too, was healed (1 Peter 2:24). Thanks to Christ, we no longer need to execute each other to be reconciled to Yahweh — if indeed we ever did.

Nor is there any need to execute our fellow men and women in order to control crime. Every single study that I am aware of — between death penalty and non–death penalty states; before and after the abolition of capital punishment within individual states; in Texas over fifty-six years (1930 to 1986) — has shown that the death penalty does *not* in fact lower homicide rates.[5] That is why proponents of execution no longer cite a deterrent effect to support their cause: they can produce no scientific basis for such an argument. Ironically enough, the primary reason they now give for capital punishment is essentially a religious one: "an eye for an eye," the lex talionis (Exodus 21:24).

That, however, is the one part of Pentateuchal law that Jesus explicitly overturned in the Sermon on the Mount (Matthew 5:38–42). Those who base their moral choices on the lex talionis today may indeed be following religious principles of some sort — but not Christian ones.

So let us return to our original question: what would Jesus do if he were confronted with Jack C. today? For that matter, what would his Abba do?

Would they congratulate his judge for the great mercy he showed Jack by not sentencing him to the electric chair? Would Father and Son approve of making Jack spend his entire adult life behind bars? When he stumbles out of that cage at age sixty-five and soon thereafter dies a lonely death in some back alley or subway station, would they call this "freedom"?

Or would God and Christ see this as capital punishment on the installment plan, as I called it earlier?

Again: I do not seek to mitigate Jack's crime. But what if he "turned, turned from his evil ways" (see Ezekiel 33:11)? Can those who follow Jesus leave him in his prison cell for five decades as a "humane" alternative to the electric chair? Or must we not say to Jack, as our Master did, "Go now and leave your life of sin behind" (John 8:11)?

> The Lord looked down from his sanctuary on high,
>   viewed the earth from heaven,
> to hear the groans of the prisoners
>   and release those condemned to die.
>   (Psalm 102:20–21)

Questions for Reflection and Discussion

1. Reflect on "an eye for an eye." Why do you think the lex talionis continues to be one of the most frequently cited verses in the Bible? Why do you think Christ overturned only this one part of Pentateuchal law and nothing else?

2. Is it really fair of the author to compare "real" capital punishment with "death penalty on the installment plan"? How

does execution differ from spending one's entire adult life in prison from the point of view of the offender? The victim or victim's family? Society as a whole?

3. How would you feel if your child were killed? Would the execution of the murderer lessen your grief? Would you want to see the killer get "life without parole"? Would "only" twenty years behind bars satisfy you? Where were you and what was your life like twenty years ago?

FOUR

John the Baptist's Defender

Advocacy for and by Individual Inmates

✤✤✤

AFTER John the Baptist's arrest, Jesus Christ did something so courageous that it was very nearly foolhardy: he gave a speech in support of his jailbird cousin, right in the town's central marketplace (Matthew 11:7–19). Not only was John "more than a prophet," Christ told the crowd, but he was in fact "the Elijah who was to come" (Matthew 11:9, 14). Why was it so dangerous for Jesus to praise John openly? Because siding publicly with a man whom the authorities considered a political threat exposed Christ himself to arrest as a partisan rabble-rouser.

"For Herod himself had given orders to have John arrested.... For John had been saying to Herod, 'It is not lawful for you to have your brother's wife,' " Herodias (Mark 6:17–18). This complaint of John's was not simply a personal attack on Herod's private life, but a direct challenge to the legitimacy of the king's rule: if Herod's marriage to Herodias was indeed "unlawful," then no son of theirs could inherit their kingdom, thus opening the door to rival claimants to the throne. Of course King Herod had no option under these circumstances but to silence John by throwing him in the dungeon! And if his cousin Jesus made too much of a fuss, he could easily find himself in the cell next to John's.

Speaking up for individual prisoners like John the Baptist, or advocating prison reform generally, is no longer as dangerous as it was in Christ's time, thank goodness. Or at least it is not for most of us. But I happen to know a man who literally risked his own life to save me from execution, in a manner not unlike Jesus' dangerous defense of John. Since you would not be reading these lines if this man had not rescued me from the electric chair, perhaps you would like to hear our story.

In the late 1980s I was in prison in England, fighting extradition to America on death penalty charges. My lawyers told me there was no hope of escaping execution — until they obtained an affidavit from a death row prisoner in Virginia who described his existence "on the row" in gruesome detail.

Because my extradition had attracted international media attention, this man knew he was exposing himself to retaliation by helping me: U.S. courts might turn down his own appeals because they resented his highly public criticism of the American criminal justice system. Yet this convict chose to take that risk, simply to save a complete stranger: me.

And he not only saved my life — the capital murder indictment against me was dropped in 1989, thanks to his affidavit — but he also saved my soul. Because I was not swiftly executed, Jesus had time to find me in 1994. And this in turn allowed me to bring some comfort to others through my writings years later.

The man who saved my life, Joseph M. Giarratano, was no angel. But perhaps he is no devil either: like John the Baptist, that dangerous fellow who threatened King Herod's throne, Joe too might turn out to have a few redeeming qualities, if we take the time to look closely.

First, the bad news: on February 3, 1979, Joe Giarratano allegedly raped fifteen-year-old Michele Kline and then killed both her and her mother, Barbara, in Norfolk, Virginia. Joe spent the night sleeping off a drug binge next to their slashed and strangled bodies and, upon waking the next morning, fled to Florida by bus. There he turned himself in to police and confessed to the crime several times.

At his trial and later, on death row, Joe claimed that he did not remember actually murdering the Klines; that the police fed him details of the crime scene to make his confession sound plausible; and that some forensic evidence pointed to a killer other than himself.

Such belated claims of innocence are not uncommon, but Virginia's governor, L. Douglas Wilder, considered Joe's sufficiently persuasive to commute his death sentence to life in prison in 1991.[1] In the years since, Joe's repeated attempts to vindicate himself completely through DNA testing have been frustrated by the state's claims that it cannot find the lab specimen in question.[2]

Fighting for his freedom is not the only thing Joseph Giarratano has done in the last twenty-five years, however. In 1995, he became the first death row prisoner ever to write a brief that was argued before the U.S. Supreme Court — not on his own behalf, but for an illiterate fellow convict who had no lawyer. He wrote articles for publications like the *Yale Law Review* and launched a rehabilitative program for prisoners called "Peace Studies — Alternatives to Violence." Based on the writings of Gandhi, King, and Dorothy Day, it dramatically lowered the disciplinary infractions of participating inmates — and led to his transfer in 1995 from Virginia to Utah, as a potential troublemaker.[3]

Thanks to pressure from his numerous supporters, Joe has meanwhile been returned to Virginia and is now housed in one of that state's two "supermax" facilities, Red Onion State Prison. In 2004, he finally became eligible for parole.[4] And that raises the challenging question of whether Joe should be released, or whether he should be required to spend the rest of his life in prison.

In our consideration of this issue, let us assume for the moment that Joseph Giarratano did indeed kill Michele and Barbara Kline. It is true, of course, that an amazing 20 percent of those prisoners exonerated by DNA tests over the last ten years had originally confessed to police, admitting to crimes they *provably* had not committed.[5] So Joe is quite correct to argue that his repeated statements to police are not conclusive proof of his guilt. But he also spent the night of the murders sleeping next to the blood-covered victims, and this circumstance is more difficult to explain away than his confessions.

What I would like to propose here, however, is that Joe's guilt or innocence need not decide the question of his possible release after twenty-five years in prison.

There is, I would suggest, no purpose to be served by incarcerating him any longer: his presumptive victims will not come back to life, he will not learn any lesson he has not already learned, and no potential killer will be more deterred by a thirty-year stint in prison than by a twenty-five-year stay. Nor will public safety be diminished by freeing Joe, since he has obviously turned his life around and has several standing job offers from major law firms.

So the only remaining reason to keep him locked up is to repay him for the terrible harm he most likely caused. True equity would require, however, that Joe Giarratano be executed — and not just once but twice, since there were two victims. But is a strict balancing-of-the-scales the kind of justice that Jesus taught?

All of us know the answer to that question, and none of us want to apply it — not to an offense as serious as the one that Joe almost certainly committed. But on the cross, Christ showed us that even the worst criminals are not beyond his forgiveness. The "thief" whom Jesus took with him to paradise was a *lestes,* a Greek term commonly applied to men like Barabbas: violent revolutionaries, political killers, their age's counterparts to al-Qaeda members (Luke 23:42). And if a repentant terrorist was not excluded from our Savior's mercy, how can we deny the same clemency to Joe Giarratano?

Perhaps, after prayer and reflection, you will come to agree with James, that "mercy triumphs over judgment" (James 2:13). And perhaps you will then feel moved to express that mercy through action, since "faith without deeds is dead" (James 2:26). If so, you may wish to follow the example Christ left us when he spoke in support of another prisoner, John the Baptist: you could write a letter to Virginia's governor, asking for Joe's release on parole. Unlike Jesus, you would not even be endangering yourself by doing so.

And if the model that our Messiah gave us here is not enough to persuade you, perhaps you might reflect on the fact that Joe Giarratano did for me precisely what I am now asking you to do for him. A death row prisoner, the lowest of the low — and not a practicing Christian — he risked his own life to save mine. Was he wrong to do so? Should he have withheld his help and let me die in the electric chair?

The address for your letter is: Governor of Virginia, State Capitol Building, Richmond, VA 23219.

Questions for Reflection and Discussion

1. Read Paul's letter to Philemon. Here the apostle pleads with his friend Philemon to forgive a common criminal: Onesimus, Philemon's runaway slave who apparently stole something from his master (v. 18). Why do you think this letter was included in the Bible? Could you use it as a model for a letter to the governor of Virginia about Joe Giarratano?

2. According to two recent studies by University of Michigan law professor Samuel R. Gross and the *North Carolina Law Review,* "there are thousands of innocent people in prison today."[6] Since we cannot be totally certain of Joe Giarratano's guilt, can we in all fairness require him to admit that he killed Michele and Barbara Kline before considering him for parole?

3. In May of 2004, Assistant U.S. Attorney General William Moschella sent members of Congress a "views" letter that asked legislators to restrict the availability of DNA testing to prisoners trying to prove their innocence. Granting inmates the right to DNA tests "can readily result in abuse by convicted criminals," Moschella warned.[7] Only four days later, the *Richmond Times-Dispatch* reported that Virginia's state Attorney General's Office was still vehemently opposing DNA tests in the celebrated and hotly disputed case of Roger Keith Coleman, executed in 1992, even after the local prosecutor's office lifted its objections. Apparently "the state cannot allow itself to say 'Oops,'" the paper editorialized.[8]

During the same month, the U.S. Department of Justice Inspector General's Office announced that Jacqueline A. Blake, a biologist in the FBI Crime Lab, had pled guilty to "submitting falsified DNA analysis reports in more than 100 cases."[9] The Associated Press, meanwhile, reported that a confidential Oklahoma City police memorandum found "compelling circumstantial evidence" that state forensic scientist Joyce

Gilchrist "doctored trial evidence and may have destroyed hair samples that could have exonerated a man now on death row."[10]

Despite the Whitehurst investigation and congressional hearings in the mid-1990s, the FBI Crime Lab is once again subject to a major investigation, and an audit in 2001 disclosed that *half* of all state forensic laboratories are not in compliance with FBI standards.[11] In the case of Earl Washington Jr., exonerated after years on Virginia's death row, that state's forensic lab produced DNA test results that are "a scientific impossibility" and "not credible or trustworthy," the *Virginian Pilot* reported. Yet the only action by Virginia's Attorney General's Office was to seek judicial sanctions against Washington's lawyers for making public details of the investigation. As in the Coleman case, "the inescapable impression is that Virginia officials care more about protecting the legal system from embarrassment than they do about identifying [the real] murderer," the paper argued.[12]

Against this background, how do you judge the state of Virginia's contention that is it unable to find the DNA samples that Joe Giarratano wants tested? Would you trust the test result if the state now claimed to have found the missing sample?

4. How would you feel if you were wrongly convicted but could not prove your innocence? How would you deal with knowing that you will die behind bars for a crime that you did not commit, and that you are the only person who knows the truth? What would you do with your time?

FIVE

John the Baptist's Execution

Correctional Health Care

✠ ✠ ✠

M Y FRIEND Calvin T. died free. Twenty-four hours are all the state gave him — just a glimpse of light and liberty, after more than two decades in prison. But at least he did not end his life in a cage.

Calvin brought it all on himself. After being released on parole in the late 1970s, he came back to "the big house" in 1984 with a new fifty-year sentence for burglary and attempted aggravated sexual battery. This did not teach him to mend his ways, either: for the next ten years or so, he used and abused all the drugs he could find. Prison life is hell on earth, and all of us convicts must find some way to make the pain bearable.

Then, like so many inmates, Calvin too began to straighten himself out after a decade behind bars. Middle age is an effective cure for the crime bug, as the Bureau of Justice Statistics confirms: ex-prisoners forty-five years and older reoffend at a rate 41 percent lower than eighteen-to-twenty-four-year-olds.[1] In the penitentiary, those calmed-down older convicts become a stabilizing force on which guards rely to keep youngsters in check. And so it was with Calvin T.

When I met him near the end of his life, he had transferred his drug-dealing and drug-acquiring skills to the procurement of spices and garnishes that just might make the bad food in the prison's chow hall more edible. Calvin was a sight to behold at the dinner table: his eye-drop bottle contained hot sauce, a chewing tobacco can held garlic powder, a small plastic bag chopped onions, and an envelope dried chili peppers. Mustard, mayonnaise, relish, and (illegal) ketchup packs were standard, of course. And he always shared his culinary accoutrements, just as he once shared a joint.

In the end, every convict must find some such way to make his life a little better. Calvin tried to spice up the gray prison food, another man might devote his time to getting the penitentiary softball field in professional condition, still another writes articles and books. To each his own.

But we can never leave our pasts behind completely, even after time turns us into semi-respectable, more-or-less-law-abiding "old heads." For some, the parole board will not let us forget, and for others — like Calvin — wild living in younger days eventually bears evil fruit. Sharing needles with other drug-addicted prisoners years ago had given Calvin a Hepatitis C infection, and when he reached his mid-fifties, that virus moved in to claim his life.

Hepatitis C — also called Hep C, or HCV — attacks the liver and is often fatal if left untreated. However, through the use of alpha-interferon or pegelated interferon in combination with ribavarin, victims can live symptom-free for many years. These medications cost $10,000 to $15,000 a year, unfortunately, and that is what killed Calvin T.

According to a major recent investigation of HCV in the Virginia Department of Corrections, which housed Calvin, 39 percent of that state's prisoners carry the Hepatitis C virus. But "only 50 inmates out of an estimated 12,800 infected inmates," or 0.3 percent, are being treated for the disease.[2] Aggravating the problem, the report said, was that the correctional department had "designed treatment eligibility requirements capable of excluding just about everyone."[3]

"Rather than risk being required to treat large numbers of infected inmates at bankrupting costs," the *New York Times* reported, "some prisons have actually cut back on testing for disease."[4] Virginia, for instance, does not test its convict population systematically and even requires prisoners to pay for their own tests. Or, to be perfectly accurate, the tests themselves are free; but in order to get them, inmates have to see the doctor, and *that* results in a $5 "co-pay" charge.[5]

Since $5 amounts to roughly five days' worth of penitentiary wages (at the starting salary of 23 cents per hour), very few convicts request Hepatitis C or HIV/AIDS tests. And the Department of Corrections does not have to treat what it does not know about.

Until, that is, the Hep-C virus begins to win its long battle against the immune system and liver, as it did in Calvin's case. By then it is too late for the interferon and ribavarin treatment; all that is left to do at this stage is to make the process of dying more comfortable. But it is just a prisoner's life, after all.

In situations like Calvin's, one would think that the Department of Corrections would at least have the decency to release terminally ill inmates under the state's medical clemency law. Even this is too soft on crime, however. Simply in order to have a prisoner's case considered by the medical clemency board, a doctor employed by the correctional department must confirm in writing that the inmate definitely has less than ninety days left to live.

Of course very few prison doctors are willing to risk their employer's displeasure by predicting a convict's death and then having the miscreant live a little longer than expected. Still, Calvin's doctor recommended medical clemency for him in February 2004 — a request that was denied.

By May 2004 Calvin had to be transported to a hospital to have fifteen pints of fluid drained from his abdomen. On a Wednesday he was released without fanfare — amazing, how quickly the Department of Corrections can expedite paperwork if it really wants to. And the next day, Thursday, he died.

No one around here, neither inmates nor guards, will mourn Calvin's passing. He was a nothing, a nobody — just an old convict whose life and death do not matter to anyone. Not even I cared much about him; we were not close, just occasional tablemates in the chow hall.

And that, to me, is the saddest aspect of this story — the nonchalance with which all of us have accepted Calvin's death. In the New Testament, I find this same attitude reflected in the execution of John the Baptist, at the request of King Herod's daughter Salome (Mark 6:17–29). The evangelist Mark turns this incident into a wonderful set-piece that demonstrates the corruption and callousness of Palestine's ruling class, which was willing to kill a man on a whim at a drunken feast. But the great banquet at which Salome danced is not my concern — that is *your* world, the free world of wine, women, and parties. My perspective is that of John the Baptist, who is down in the dungeon and hears the music and revelry only dimly, at a great distance.

John is minding his own business down in his cell, keeping to himself like every convict should. Then he hears steps approaching, and the door clanks open. "Step out," a guard calls, and John complies.

Is it freedom at last? No. The guard who unlocked the door is in fact the executioner, sent by King Herod. Without explanation, the man pulls his sword — and a blink of an eye later, John's head falls to the floor.

The executioner feels neither malice nor joy: this is simply his job, and John is just another prisoner, after all. No one mourns an old convict's passing.

His death means nothing. Nothing at all.

Questions for Reflection and Discussion

1. In the Gospel of Mark, we read that after John the Baptist's execution, his disciples "came and took his body and laid it in a tomb" (Mark 6:29). Thus King Herod's malevolence apparently did not extend to denying deceased convicts a proper burial, considered essential in first-century Palestine. In modern-day Virginia, by contrast, the Department of Corrections will not even provide accurate information about prisoner deaths, never mind making decent funeral arrangements. According to the report cited in this chapter,

   While statistics on the [Virginia Department of Corrections'] website claim that no inmates died of Hepatitis in 2001, results of autopsies performed by the Office of the

Medical Examiner of Virginia show that at least seven inmates died of Hepatitis in 2001.

Classifying all information about the deaths of prisoners as "medical records," the Virginia Department of Corrections employs a combination of exclusions to the Virginia Freedom of Information Act to withhold almost all information about such deaths, including post-mortem reports on how medical treatment was handled, the names of prisoners who died, and the causes of deaths.[6]

Reflect on the cultural and religious differences between first-century Palestine and twenty-first century America. Why did King Herod, a petty tyrant, show so much more respect for a dead prisoner than the Virginia Department of Corrections does? Is it possible that Herod's attitude was at least in part due to the fact that John the Baptist had friends who cared enough about him to claim his body, whereas deceased convicts today usually have no family ties, no one to give them a dignified funeral? Might this be an unusual but worthwhile area for a new prison ministry?

2. "By failing to confront public health problems [like HCV] in prison," the *New York Times* noted, "this country could be setting itself up for new epidemics down the line."[7] "If we don't treat the prisoners inside the prison, we'll have to pay twice as much to treat the complications of their diseases after they're released," according to Laura LaFay, the author of the report cited in this chapter.[8] But consider the following: if the Virginia Department of Corrections' HCV infection rate of 39 percent were to be extrapolated to all 2.2 million of America's inmates, then 819,000 prisoners would require treatment at a cost of $10,000 to $15,000 per year — a total medical bill of $8.19 to $12.3 billion annually. Those figures do not include treatment costs for HIV/AIDS, another enormous epidemiological problem in correctional facilities nationwide. What is really affordable in this area?

3. When contacted about the Hepatitis C report cited in this chapter, Larry Traylor, spokesperson for the Virginia Department of Corrections, said that "inmates receive the same community standard of care [as other Virginians]. Oftentimes they receive better medical care than they received on the street."[9] Since most prisoners come from extreme low-income backgrounds, it is probably true that many do receive better health services in the penitentiary than before their arrests. However, "community standard of care" is a technical term used by doctors to describe the minimum level of care, including specific treatment protocols, for individual diseases. And the "community" whose "standard" is to be applied is not that of inner-city ghettos, but of all Americans — so the medical profession says.

Do you think inmates should be given the same quality of treatment as law-abiding citizens? Would you make some exceptions, such as organ transplants? How about expensive cancer therapies for prisoners who will never be released? Where would you draw the line?

The Good Samaritan

Prison Rape

✠✠✠

ICANNOT even remember what I screamed, so scared was I. But it must have been unusually persuasive, for Flickin' Joe loosened his grip just enough for me to slide out of his hold, scamper away from the showers, and lock myself in my cell. Somewhere on the top tier I left behind my soap dish and my shampoo, my towel and my dignity — but not, thank goodness, my virginity.

Flickin' Joe must have been stalking me for months. Like the rest of the inmates and the guards, I had assumed he was no danger to men because his primary sexual outlet was "gunning down" female correctional officers. That was how he had earned his nickname: when a woman guard came into view, he would busily flick himself with his middle finger through his skin-tight shorts. Neither the staff nor other prisoners dared object because Flickin' Joe had the physique of a professional weightlifter and the temper of a pit bull with a hangover. I figured that a young, white "fresh fish" like me was out of the firing line. Was I ever wrong!

Such was my personal introduction to penitentiary love, fourteen years ago (at the time of this writing) in Mecklenburg Correctional Center in Boydton, Virginia. At that point I had already spent nearly four years in jail in England, whence I had unsuccessfully fought extradition to the United States. Inmate-on-inmate rapes were unknown in the London prison where I had been housed; even consensual homosexuality was rare and frowned-upon. In America, on the other hand, the "convict code" encourages both forced and unforced sex, as I nearly learned at Flickin' Joe's tender hands.

My first reaction upon reaching the safety of my cell was relief so intense that it swept through my body like a wave. Feeling another man pressed against my back, sensing nothing between me and penetration but the ultra-thin fabric of his sports shorts, knowing that my attacker outweighed me by over a hundred pounds, seeing the correctional officer in the dayroom control booth discreetly look down at her *National Enquirer,* realizing that no other prisoner would prevent Flickin' Joe from breaking in the new guy, and hearing him growl in my ear, "What choo gonna do if I drag you in my cell *right now?*" — all this was perhaps the single most frightening experience of my life. Once the terror passed, I felt both exhausted and strangely elated. I had lived to fight another day! But then I began to realize that my problems were far from over. In some ways, in fact, they had just begun.

At the reception and classification center where I had spent a few months before coming to this prison, I and at least a dozen other new intakes had watched a young man get raped. His cell partner pulled a homemade knife on him and forced him to perform fellatio through a broken-out window in their cell door on a prisoner in the hallway. Everyone — including myself, I am sorry to say — cheered and applauded, perhaps because we were all so intensely relieved that we were not the ones being abused.

When the victim reported the assault, he was placed in the punishment block "for his own protection," while the aggressor remained in the general prison population. No one dared to cooperate with the perfunctory institutional investigation, since snitches were beaten, raped, and sometimes killed. And so the predator was never held accountable at all, while his victim could look forward to spending his entire sentence "protected" in a series of punitive segregation units.

Knowing this, I did not tell the guards about Flickin' Joe's attack on me. Nor did I speak to the facility's psychologist: he simply doled out tranquilizers and, in any case, would report the assault to security staff. If I turned to other inmates for emotional support, they would read this sign of weakness as an invitation to become my "prison daddy" or "friend" — both penitentiary euphemisms for jailhouse husbands. Telling my family was out of the question, too, since that would only cause them anxiety about something they could not change. So I kept my mouth firmly shut and started lifting weights to work off my pent-up emotions.

Looking back, I realize how freakishly, almost unbelievably lucky I was that I had not been raped, like so many other fresh fish. Had I been, I might well be dead today, since Flickin' Joe died of AIDS eight or nine years ago. That is the part of the story that late-night comedians leave out when they crack jokes about dropping the soap in a penitentiary shower.

Because the overwhelming majority of male rape victims are convicted criminals, however, "the only people who care are the relatives [of the incarcerated victims], and they are usually poor and uneducated," explains Cal Skinner Jr., a Republican state representative from Illinois. He blames his efforts to introduce prison rape prevention legislation for his defeat in the 2000 elections.[1]

Why should you care any more than former representative Skinner's voters? Because, as we also saw in chapter 2, the HIV infection rate of prisoners in New York's correctional system, for instance, is *almost thirty times* as high as the civilian rate (8.5 percent vs. 0.3 percent). Thus, at an average annual cost of $8,000 to $12,000 per infected inmate, the financial consequences of HIV/AIDS in America's prisons are enormous.[2] The bad news does not end with your wallet, however: of America's 2.2 million convicts, 625,000 are released every year,[3] some of them as undiagnosed carriers of HIV/AIDS.

And there is still more bad news: while I am unaware of any academic research on this subject, numerous conversations with other convicts have persuaded me that prison rape plays a significant role in this country's shamefully high recidivism rate of 67.5 percent.[4]

Meet "Pissed-off Pete," an acquaintance of mine at my current prison. In 1982, when he was twenty and "soft," he was raped by two older convicts in their facility's "honor dorm," a housing unit for especially well-behaved prisoners. Pete dealt with his pain by smoking marijuana — something he had done only rarely before the assault — and by getting into as many fights as possible to prove his manhood to himself and others.

In 1993, Pete made parole and settled down to a good, nine-to-five job. But for the last eleven years, he had solved all his problems through cannabis and fisticuffs, and old habits like that are hard to break. So by 1995 he was back behind bars for failing a urinalysis test and committing a misdemeanor assault.

Ironically enough, one of Pete's rapists from 1982 is now at the same prison with us and is about to be released upon completing his sentence. Pete himself, on the other hand, must expect to serve many more years for violating the parole granted to him in 1993.

Whenever Pete is released, the family to which he will return will look much like yours. Many convicts, and therefore many prison rape victims, are not hardened criminals at all. At present, one quarter of all inmates are serving time for so-called "drug-only" offenses,[5] while another 11 percent are locked up for "public order" crimes like drunk driving.[6] An increasing number of these prisoners are college students, realtors, small business owners, aerospace engineers, and church ministers — to cite the backgrounds of just five of my acquaintances at my current penitentiary. To the predators, these middle-class white folk are ideal victims.

One of these fellow prisoners of mine, Henry, once owned and operated a Pilates studio. When his cellmate gave him the choice of providing smokes or "booty" (i.e., anal sex), this fifty-year-old gentleman refused to return to their cell, whereupon the guards placed him in the punishment block, for "Disciplinary Offense 201 — Disobeying an Order." That in-house conviction for breaking prison rules will extend the overall time Henry must serve by several months, due to loss of good behavior credits. And upon leaving the punitive segregation unit, he will be lucky to face only verbal harassment by the inmate on whom he snitched. In a slightly tougher medium security penitentiary, Henry would definitely get *hurt*.

But Henry is lucky: he was charged only with the single offense of disobeying an order. When prisoners make allegations of sexual assault, correctional officers will sometimes tell the victim that he can leave the protection of the punishment block only if he gives a written statement that his rape allegation was untrue.

This devil's bargain begins to sound attractive after a month or two in punitive segregation — especially to a fresh fish. But signing such a statement allows the guards to charge the victim with "Disciplinary Offense 206 — Lying and Giving False Information," a not-uncommon occurrence.

Most victims of inmate-on-inmate rape are not middle-aged white men like Henry, of course, for the simple reason that young African Americans are the largest demographic group behind prison walls. On every rec yard in every penitentiary in the United States, there is always a "sistahood" or "girl's choir" of exaggeratedly effeminate young black men who wear rouge and lipstick, carry purses, and call each other by names like Jazz, Ophelia or Kiki. They have been "turned out" by older, tougher convicts — in effect, driven insane by years of continuous sexual victimization. In chapter 2, we met one such unfortunate creature: Oliver/Olivia, who attempted to castrate himself with a razor blade and wrote in blood on the cell wall, "I am a woman."

In my experience, it is not so much race as perceived weakness that leads to being raped in prison. Wolves of all races prey on the young, the old, and the mentally ill. Of the 14,500 juveniles who are tried as adults each year and sent to adult correctional centers,[7] for instance, virtually all become "punks," or sex slaves. One such youngster whom I will never forget eventually took on the name "Baby-doll" and charged $1.09 for oral sex, the price (at that time) of a pack of Doral cigarettes and two packs of iced tea mix.

Of the 400,000 mentally ill offenders currently housed in U.S. prisons, most are mixed into the general convict population and earn their cigarette money by performing fellatio in the porta-toilets in the rec yards. At my current facility, this practice has earned the porta-toilet the nickname "the love shack." One-stop shoppers often purchase the mentally ill inmates' saved-up psychotropic medication after sex, for a nice little postcoital "buzz."

If asked, the mentally ill inmates practicing free enterprise in the love shack would probably deny that they are sexually and financially exploited and might well resent any attempt to eliminate this income-earning opportunity. And that points up one of the major difficulties in combating prison rape: the culture of denial among convicts themselves.

According to the Virginia Department of Corrections, there are roughly a dozen rapes reported each year among its 31,000 inmates,[8] so its spokesperson could accurately claim that this problem "was not widespread."[9] But national statistics suggest that closer to 6,200 forced sexual encounters, including 3,100 actual rapes, would occur annually in a correctional population of that size.

Why the divergence? Because of the realities of prison life: rape has become such an integral part of penitentiary culture that most convicts and even guards no longer recognize it as wrong. When a young, clearly retarded white man recently arrived at my current facility, established inmates and officers joked about forming a betting pool for who would claim him — or "her," as he was already being referred to. A black old-timer took an early lead, spending hours on the rec yard with his prospective punk. But to everyone's surprise, a tall white inmate nicknamed "Country" ended up winning the competition for "Mrs. Country," as his new wife is now known.

Of course no other prisoner sought to protect the fresh fish, because that would have put his potential rescuer in conflict with the predators. If I had arranged to have this young man moved into my own cell, for instance, everyone on the compound would have assumed that he was now *my* sex slave. And I would probably have been forced to defend my "property" against challengers.

Correctional officers of all ranks add another layer of denial of the problem. According to a former warden in the Oklahoma Department of Corrections, "prison rape to a large degree is made more serious by the deliberate indifference of most prison officials. Oftentimes these officials will purposefully turn their back on unspeakable acts in order to maintain 'peace.' "[10] "Rapes, beatings and servitude are the currency of power" behind bars, U.S. District Judge William Wayne Justice found in *Ruiz v. Estelle,* a class-action case about Texas prison conditions. To gain the cooperation of inmate leaders, "prison officials deliberately resist providing reasonable safety to [weak] inmates. The result is that individual prisoners who seek protection from their attackers are either not believed, disregarded, or told that there is a lack of evidence to support action by the prison system."[11]

I observed one especially egregious example of this phenomenon several years ago, at a different facility: my housing unit's "tier boss" gave the sergeant in charge a carton of Marlboro cigarettes in exchange for having a punk nicknamed Crowbar placed in his cell. Normally, no such bribe would have been necessary. But Crowbar had deliberately broken a rule in order to be sent to the punishment block and thus to escape this tier boss. So to have him moved back specifically into his persecutor's cell required a little extra . . . lubrication.

As in virtually all such situations, none of the associated Department of Corrections paperwork gave any hint of rape. When one man beats another into submission to force sex on him, guards will at most write him up for "Disciplinary Offense 218 — Fighting with Any Person," a minor ("200-series") infraction that can be processed in a few minutes. Charging the aggressor with "Disciplinary Offense 106-b — Sexual Assault or Making Forcible Sexual Advances Toward an Inmate" involves far more paperwork and the officer's attendance at the subsequent disciplinary hearing. As a result, my current facility has not had a single *officially recorded* instance of rape in years, though I am aware of a dozen undocumented cases of forced sex within the last few months.

One hopeful sign on the horizon is the Prison Rape Elimination Act, signed into law on September 4, 2003. Co-sponsored in Congress by Representatives Frank R. Wolf, R-Va., and Robert C. Scott, D-Va., as well as Senators Edward M. Kennedy, D-Mass., and Jeff Sessions, R-Ala.,[12] this bill calls on states to gather reliable statistics on the issue, encourages the development of prevention strategies, and creates a review panel to hold annual hearings.[13] But, while this measure at least recognizes this tragic phenomenon, I doubt it can break the code of silence that has kept sexual assault behind bars hidden for so long.

As far as administrative remedies are concerned, there are some correctional facilities that could serve as models for reform nationwide. San Francisco's jail system instituted procedures as long ago as 1975 that provide for the separate housing of weak-looking and effeminate prisoners, and the California Department of Corrections makes at least a minimal attempt to protect new inmates for the first sixty days after their arrival at classification units. Because it does so by placing prisoners of the same race in one cell, however, the latter policy is now under review by the U.S. Supreme Court.[14]

What I think is more likely to bring real change in the area of prison rape prevention is lawsuits by the incarcerated victims' family members. The mother of a convict who committed suicide at the Lake County, Illinois, jail recently won $1.75 million from Correctional Medical Services and the jail for not taking adequate precautionary measures in view of her son's known mental illness.[15] While there was no suggestion of rape in that case, similar deliberate indifference and negligence arguments could be mounted in the suicides of weak or effeminate-looking prisoners who make documented complaints of sexual abuse, are ignored by staff, and then kill themselves. A few six-figure damage awards would certainly get the attention of departments of correction.

At last, wardens and guards would have a real incentive to end the culture of silence that currently protects Flickin' Joe and his ilk. The correctional officer in the control booth at Mecklenburg Correctional Center, for instance, certainly saw Joe grab me as I came out of the shower, but she simply had no reason to stop reading her *National Enquirer.* If her job had depended on preventing a possible million-dollar jury award, however, she would have radioed for help immediately. And I might have been spared Flickin' Joe's loving embrace.

Unfortunately, the overwhelming majority of prisoners — including me — do not have family members willing to send them $10 at Christmas, much less to hire an attorney after they are raped. We are alone and helpless; no one in your world even knows our names, much like the anonymous "man who fell victim to robbers" in Christ's parable of the good Samaritan (see Luke 10:29–37; 30). If the victim is invisible — hidden in a roadside ditch, locked away in a jail — it is so very easy for good people to shut their ears to cries of help!

That the good Samaritan took the time to investigate those calls from the ditch is amazing enough, given the natural human inclination to ignore the problems of others. What makes him a model of Christian charity, however, is that he reached out to *help an "enemy."* Since he was traveling on the road "from Jerusalem to Jericho," the Samaritan knew that whoever was calling out to him was almost certainly a Jew, a member of a hostile religious and ethnic group (Luke 10:30). Samaritans despised Jews as much as Jews despised Samaritans — and perhaps as much as law-abiding citizens despise convicted felons in the United States today.

Yet the Samaritan did not say to himself, "That Jew deserved what he got!" Instead, he provided medical treatment ("bandaged ...his wounds"), transportation ("lifted him up on his own animal"), personal attention ("cared for him"), and even professional aftercare by the innkeeper ("gave [him] two silver coins") (Luke 10:34–35). By surmounting the social barrier between Jew and Samaritan with an act of practical charity, the hero of this parable thus did precisely what the Son of God had done in his many healing miracles.

An often overlooked fact of Christ's supernatural cures is that he bestowed so many of them on marginalized members of society. Thanks to their gender, the woman with a hemorrhage and the crippled woman were second-class citizens at best, and those in the advanced stages of leprosy were pariahs who had to stand at a distance from healthy folk like Jesus (Luke 9:43, 13:10–17, 5:12–16, 17:11–9). Not only did our Savior restore them to health, but he spoke to each of them individually and even touched them. This human contact, this laying on of his hands, probably meant as much to the sick women and lepers as their actual cures (Luke 13:13). For the first time, perhaps, they were no longer outcasts but full human beings who could be touched without inspiring revulsion.

Those inmates who have been raped behind bars are no less in need of healing hands than the robbery victim in the parable of the good Samaritan or victims of sexual assault in your world, for that matter. Even if you do not feel a call to this particularly difficult ministry, however, you can still help these men and women. Contact the volunteer organization Stop Prisoner Rape, 3325 Wilshire

Blvd., Ste. 340, Los Angeles, CA 90010 (*www.spr.org*). There are still some good Samaritans out there, and they could surely use your "two silver coins."

Questions for Reflection and Discussion

1. Under the Mosaic code, people who knowingly exposed others to mortal danger were subject to the death penalty:

   > If an ox was previously in the habit of goring people and its owner, though warned, would not keep it in; should it then kill a man or woman, not only must the ox be stoned, but its owner also must be put to death. (Exodus 21:29)

   Given the prevalence of HIV/AIDS among convicts, prison rape is a danger no less mortal — and no less known — than the habitually homicidal ox cited above. So should the principle of Exodus 21:29 be applied to correctional administrators who deliberately ignore rape behind bars "in order to maintain 'peace'"?

2. In the civilian world, tort claims are often adjudicated under the familiar "negligence" standard. But the Prison Litigation Reform Act of 1996 (PLRA) requires a different, much higher standard for suits brought by inmates: "deliberate indifference," which requires prisoners to prove that correctional administrators *knowingly* ignored a *specific* danger. By raising procedural requirements for convict-plaintiffs to near-impossible heights, Congress succeeded in filtering out most nuisance lawsuits by inmates — at the cost of also barring many justified court actions. Virginia state senator Henry Marsh III, D-Richmond, recently submitted legislation to exempt prison rape cases in that state from the PLRA's hurdles, but his bill was defeated. According to state senator Mark Obenshain, R-Harrisonburg, "The creativity of folks with a lot of time on their hands, especially when they don't have to pay for it, is boundless."[16]

Given what you have read in this chapter, do you think many inmates would risk ridicule and retaliation from other convicts by filing a prison-rape lawsuit, *unless* that claim were genuine? If not, why do you think legislators like Senator Obenshain oppose changing the PLRA?

3. In July of 2002, the U.S. Congress held hearings on the Prison Rape Elimination Act (then called Prison Rape Reduction Act). One witness was the mother of sixteen-year-old Texas inmate Rodney Hulin, who committed suicide after being raped by other prisoners.[17] Why do you think she was willing to testify in public about her son's fate, unlike the hundreds of thousands (!) of other mothers whose sons are sexually assaulted behind bars each year? Would you be willing to appear on C-SPAN to discuss your child's criminal history and his or her subsequent rape by other inmates?

SEVEN

The Persistent Widow and the Unjust Judge

Parole Abolition

✠✠✠

T HE EIGHTEENTH CHAPTER of the Gospel of Luke begins with one of those little scriptural pearls that spiritual piggies like me often trot past on our way to meatier biblical passages: the parable of the persistent widow and the unjust judge. Because we so frequently skip over this teaching tale in favor of the next parable, about the Pharisee and the Tax Collector praying in the synagogue, let us recall what the text actually says:

> Jesus told his disciples a parable to show them that they should always pray and not give up. He said: "In a certain town there was a judge who neither feared God nor cared about men. And there was a widow in that town who kept coming to him with the plea, 'Grant me justice against my adversary.' For some time he refused. But finally he said to himself, 'Even though I don't fear God or care about men, yet because this widow keeps bothering me, I will see that she gets justice, so that she won't eventually wear me out [or: strike me]' " (Luke 18:1–5).

The central message here is deceptively straightforward: pray hard and God will give you what you want. No doubt it is the apparent simplicity of this lesson that leads us to ignore the parable of the persistent widow much as the judge initially ignored her. What I would like to suggest here, however, is that there is more to this story than the obvious point about perseverance in prayer suggests.

To begin with, let us examine the metaphor that Christ used in this parable: an *unjust* judge. This is not one that would immediately come to mind in twenty-first-century America, which has come to regard judges and courts with the kind of respect and near-religious awe that used to be reserved for church figures. In our age and culture, we even let Supreme Court justices decide presidential elections! The idea that these hallowed figures on the bench might in some cases be "unjust," as Jesus takes for granted in our parable here, strikes most of us as very nearly blasphemous.

Yet both our Old and New Testaments take a much more critical view of human judges. In Psalm 82, "God ... gives judgment among the 'gods': 'How long will you judge unjustly and favor the cause of the wicked? Defend the cause of the weak and fatherless; maintain the rights of the poor and oppressed' " (Psalm 82:1–3). Some scholars take the "gods" in this psalm to mean pagan deities, over whom Yahweh exercises some sort of authority. But in every other Old Testament passage in which God exhorts his listeners to "defend the cause of the weak and the fatherless," that command is directed to humans, not pagan deities. So the most plausible reading of this psalm is as a critique of human judges who are so self-righteous that the author lampoons them as "gods."

In the New Testament, this same critical attitude toward judges is reflected in Jesus' advice to "settle matters quickly with your adversary who is taking you to court," because the legal system is self-evidently merciless: "the judge [will] turn you over to the officer, and the officer [will] throw you into prison. I tell you, you will not get out until you have paid the last penny" (Matthew 5:25–26; Luke 12:58–59). In *The Powers That Be,* renowned theologian and biblical scholar Walter Wink gives us historical insight into the scenario Christ describes:

> Indebtedness was a plague in first-century Palestine. Jesus' parables are full of debtors struggling to salvage their lives.... Exorbitant interest (25 to 250 percent) could be used to drive landowners ever deeper into debt ... to pry Galilean peasants

loose from their land. By the time of Jesus we see this process already far advanced: large estates owned by absentee landlords, managed by stewards, and worked by tenant farmers, day laborers and slaves.[1]

Thus early Christians, mostly lower-class men and women, saw courts and judges primarily as tools of their oppressors. And given that background, the "unjust judge" in Jesus' parable of the persistent widow would have been seen as a common fact of his listeners' lives.

If we take a far more reverential attitude toward judges in our own age, that is not necessarily a reflection of the much-improved quality of twenty-first-century legal training and ethics. More probably, we have simply lost touch with the roots of our faith, a religion originally meant for "the foolish, . . . the weak, . . . the lowly . . . and the despised" (1 Corinthians 1:26–30). But upon further reflection we have to admit that Christ may have a point: even American judges are human, so they must be subject to temptations and prejudices. And if the possibility that they might be "unjust" is too sacrilegious to suggest ourselves, we need only take the word of U.S. Supreme Court Justice Anthony M. Kennedy.

On August 10, 2003, he gave a speech on the need for sentencing reform at the American Bar Association's general assembly. There Justice Kennedy told his listeners, "Our resources are misspent, our punishments too severe, our sentences too long. . . . In too many cases, [long sentences] are unjust."[2]

That is a fairly stunning admission for any professional to make about one of the central elements of his or her own vocation, so perhaps we should spend a few minutes examining the excessively long prison sentences that Justice Kennedy considers so unjust. These are, in fact, one of the two major reasons why the U.S. correctional population expanded so dramatically in the last thirty years, from 300,000 in the 1970s to 2.2 million today.[3] "From the mid-1980s to the early 1990s, prison growth was driven most forcefully by the war on drugs," according to a new study. But "in the 1990s, the primary cause of prison growth . . . became longer sentences rather than more prison admissions."[4]

Keeping offenders locked up for decades on end is not an effective crime prevention strategy, however, because crime is essentially a young man's game. "Most men age out of committing violent crimes in their 30s," notes New York City Corrections Commissioner Michael Jacobson. "It is difficult to say you are preventing crime by locking up men in their 50s, 60s and 70s."[5]

Yet more and more elderly inmates are filling this country's prisons: today's figure of 125,000 is expected to rise to *one-third* of the total correctional population by 2030.[6] And since higher medical expenses mean that incarceration costs for an older prisoner are three times as high as for a younger one, health care expenses for elderly convicts in California, for instance, will amount to $5 *billion* by 2020 — the entire prison budget for 2002.[7]

Thus the overlong sentences criticized by Justice Kennedy are not only "unjust," but also unnecessary for preventing crime and fiscally harmful to states already struggling with budgetary crises. What then shall we do? Oddly enough, the Old Testament gives us very specific counsel about this precise issue, in two different places:

> But if men are bound in chains,
>   held fast by cords of affliction,
> [God] tells them what they have done —
>   that they have sinned arrogantly. . . .
> If they obey and serve him,
>   they will spend the rest of their days in prosperity
>   and their years in contentment.   (Job 36:8–11)

> Some sat in darkness and the deepest gloom,
>   prisoners suffering in iron chains,
> for they had rebelled against the words of God
>   and despised the counsel of the Most High. . . .
> Then they cried to the Lord in their trouble,
>   and he saved them from their distress.
> He brought them out of darkness and deepest gloom,
>   and broke away their chains.   (Psalm 107:10–14)

If they do not listen and repent, they will of course "die without knowledge"; but who would have thought that *reformed* prisoners, at least, are supposed to have their chains "broken away" (Job 36:12; Psalm 107:14)?

In the New Testament, we do not find such explicit directions on criminal justice issues. Yet Paul made very clear that restoring offenders to the community, not excluding them forever, was to be the ultimate goal of punishment within the church:

> Brothers, if someone is caught in a sin, you who are spiritual should restore him gently. But watch yourself, or you also may be tempted.... (Galatians 6:1)

> The punishment inflicted on him by the majority is sufficient for him. Now instead, you ought to forgive and comfort him, so that he will not be overwhelmed by excessive sorrow. I urge you, therefore, to reaffirm your love for him. (2 Corinthians 2:6–8)

Whether criminals should be treated with the same compassion that Paul counsels here for errant church members is certainly debatable. But it might be wise to "watch yourself, or you also may be tempted" when we advocate harsh sentencing policies like those criticized by Justice Kennedy.

Instead of laying down general principles as Paul did in the epistles above, Jesus preferred to teach through parables, anecdotes, and stories taken from real life. So perhaps we should take a look at what the parable of the persistent widow and the unjust judge might sound like today. As it happens, I know a widow in her seventies named Ann, now remarried, whom Christ would surely have immortalized in a teaching tale if he had met her two thousand years ago.

Ann's son, Jim, was a troubled youth whose Attention Deficit and Hyperactivity Disorder (ADHD) got him in trouble with the law throughout his teens. At seventeen, he was tried as an adult and finally sent to a real, grown-up prison. There he served twenty-two years for burglary, aggravated assault, and aggravated sexual battery.

Last year, at age forty, Jim finished all his prison sentences for those crimes — but he was not released. Instead, he will have to serve *another* thirteen years behind bars, because a judge reimposed a previously suspended prison sentence for a burglary Jim committed at age seventeen. This practice is perfectly legal, very common, and politically popular: "lock 'em up and throw away the key!"

Because Jim was originally tried in 1980, before the abolition of parole, Ann is allowed to go to the parole board every other year or so to plead for her son's freedom. The board is not listening, however: in spite of Jim's exemplary conduct in prison, they send her the same preprinted rejection notice after each parole hearing. Her son cannot be released "due to the serious nature and circumstances of the offense," the papers all say.

The only offense for which Jim is now serving time, you will recall, is that single burglary from twenty-three years ago — a burglary in which *nothing was taken,* by the way. A troubled kid's stupid adventure.

Since nothing can change the "serious nature and circumstances" of that burglary, Ann has no realistic chance of getting Jim out of prison. Virginia, the state in which she lives and her son is serving time, grants early release to only 2 percent of the thousands of aging convicts like Jim, who are still technically eligible for parole but have a violent crime in their past.[8] "We assume that the judge did not intend for them to be released," said Virginia's parole board chairperson Helen Fahey to explain why older prisoners are being kept behind bars for so long.[9] The contrary is true, however: the judges who imposed sentences decades ago, before parole abolition, never imagined that the criminals they were sending to jail would be kept there until the bitter end.

In spite of the apparent hopelessness of her and Jim's situation, Ann keeps going to the parole board each time they schedule one of their futile hearings. "Grant me justice," she pleads, just like the persistent widow (Luke 18:3). And every time the unjust judge gives her the same answer: "due to the serious nature and circumstances.... "

The lesson of the parable of the persistent widow and the unjust judge is that we should pray hard and never give up, so I would like to ask you to join your prayers with Ann's and ask God to restore her son to her. For some of us — including, I must admit, myself — it might seem a little strange or even presumptuous to ask for God's direct and practical intervention in a worldly matter like a parole decision. Prayer is supposed to be a spiritual act, after all: a way to conform our will to our Father's, not to persuade him to see things our way. But perhaps Christ deliberately chose to explain prayer in terms of a widow pestering a judge in order to encourage us to see the social and even political dimensions of prayer.

According to Walter Wink in *The Powers That Be*, cited earlier, "Prayer is never a private inner act disconnected from day-to-day realities. It is, rather, the interior battlefield where the decisive victory is won before any engagement in the outer world is even possible."[10] In our parable, we can well imagine how the widow fought on that "interior battlefield" of prayer each time the unjust judge denied her plea. What gave her the power to return time after time, to give her cause yet one more try in spite of all the disappointments that went before? Surely she must have been praying intensely all along!

And God answered the widow's prayers, not by miraculously changing the judge's mind and thereby interfering in his free will, but by giving her the strength to persist until she persuaded the judge. Thus prayer transformed a lonely little old lady, one of the most powerless members of society, into a potent agent for achieving justice, one of the primary hallmarks of our Father's kingdom. Who would dare to refuse to call *that* a miracle?

Perhaps the same miracle will happen in your life as you pray for "my" persistent widow, Ann, and her son, Jim. Perhaps, if you pray hard enough, your prayer will propel you out of your chair and into the public arena, where you will support officials like Supreme Court Justice Kennedy in their efforts to end overlong prison sentences. Perhaps you, like the widow of the parable, will pester unjust judges to adopt the Pauline approach to justice: while criminals must be punished, they should not be "overwhelmed by excessive sorrow" either (2 Corinthians 2:7). Perhaps.

It all depends on how hard you pray.

> I cry to you, Lord,
>   I say, You are my refuge,
>   my portion in the land of the living. . . .

Lead me out of my prison
　　that I may give thanks to your name.
Then the just shall gather around me
　　because you have been good to me.
　　　　　　　　　　　　(Psalm 142:6, 8)

Questions for Reflection and Discussion

1. In the letter of James, we find yet another New Testament reference to the court system being used by the rich to exploit the poor (James 2:6). Imagine the scene at the "love feasts" of the early church, described by James, as oppressors and oppressed sat together — but now, surprisingly, with the poor in the place of honor and the rich at the foot of the table. Where did judges fit into this seating arrangement? On the one hand, they did the dirty work of the wealthy landowners, but on the other hand, they were little better than servants themselves. In our own age and society, whose interests do judges serve? Whose interests does someone like Virginia Parole Board Chairperson Helen Fahey serve?

2. Every few months, the media report on another gruesome murder committed by someone on parole or probation. How would you feel if one of your relatives were killed by a parolee? Do you think that parole policies generally should be determined by the victims of parolees who reoffend after release? If not, on what criteria should parole policies be based?

3. Reflect on the social dimension of prayer. How does prayer "work"? Do you tell God what to do, does God tell you what to do, does God tell others to do what you want done? How can prayer change the world around you? How can it move the heart of an unjust judge?

EIGHT

The Judgment of the Nations

The Civil Commitment of Sex Offenders

✠✠✠

O N January 13, 2004, between 10:30 and 11:00 p.m., an acquaintance of mine was murdered. His cellmate strangled him to death in Sussex I State Prison in Waverly, Virginia. My acquaintance's name was Richard Alvin Ausley, and he was a child molester.

Some would say that Ausley finally got his just deserts. In 1961, he kidnapped and sexually assaulted a ten-year-old boy and left him tied up in the woods, a crime for which he spent ten years in prison. Twelve years later, he abducted a thirteen-year-old boy named Paul Martin Andrews, raped him numerous times, and buried him alive in a box in a rural part of Virginia. Incredibly enough, Ausley kidnapped Andrews on the very day he was to have appeared in a Portsmouth, Virginia, court for the brutal rape of another teenager.[1] Andrews fortunately was rescued by hunters after eight days, and Ausley was sentenced to forty-eight years in prison.[2]

In 2003, Ausley was scheduled for release. Because he had been sentenced in 1973, long before the abolition of parole in Virginia in 1995, his forty-eight-year sentence was completed after just thirty years. The Department of Corrections was legally required to set him free.

Informed by a former detective, Paul Andrews quite understandably launched a campaign to prevent his tormentor's return to society.[3] The solution, Andrews explained on NBC's *The Today*

Show in 2003, was to have Ausley civilly committed — that is, to confine him in a state mental hospital as a violent sexual predator.

But Richard Ausley was never committed to a psychiatric facility. Instead, he was sent to a high security prison for especially disruptive inmates and placed in a cell with a convict who had himself been molested as a child. Shortly afterward, Ausley was dead.

In the early years of this century, Ausley and I were both incarcerated at a medium security facility: Brunswick Correctional Center in Lawrenceville, Virginia. We were not friends by any stretch of the imagination, but I had several interactions with him. Prisons are like small villages: everyone knows everyone else, if only through borrowing cigarettes off each other.

Like Ausley, I too am a high-profile inmate. My 1989 extradition from England set a legal precedent still found in law books today; my 1990 trial was featured on *The Geraldo Rivera Show* ahead of the Menendez brothers' case; and fictionalized versions of the crime of which I was convicted are still broadcast as reruns on CourtTV, Discovery Channel, and A&E. So I know a little of what Ausley felt as his past was replayed in the media over and over and over again.

On the other hand, I am alleged to have killed my girlfriend's parents because — so she claimed — her mother had sexually abused and taken nude photographs of her, which the mother then showed to friends. Whether my girlfriend's mother did in fact abuse her is as much in dispute as my supposed guilt as the murderer; I claim I only covered up the crime after the fact.[4] But whatever my actual role may have been, my *motive* included loathing of child molesters. So I have considerable sympathy with Richard Ausley's victim, Paul Andrews, as well. If there is any bright side to this dark story, it is his success in leading a normal, productive life despite the unspeakable suffering he had to endure as a child.

But I cannot just dismiss Ausley as a monster, if for no other reason than that I knew the man. One day, when the civil commitment storm was raging at its fiercest in the newspapers, he came to my table in the chow hall, asked to sit down, and said to me, "I just don't know what to do. You know what I mean. Can you help me?"

I certainly did know what he meant, and I knew I could not help him. I told him so, and he shuffled away: a wizened, frail man in his mid-sixties, barely five feet tall, and — to be frank — more than a little crazy after three decades in prison. It was one of the last times I saw him alive.

Now, when I look back on it, I regret that I let Ausley walk away from my table without at least trying to help him somehow. I could not have prevented his murder, I know, but I failed him as a fellow human being. Perhaps this chapter will in some small way make up for that failure of mine in the chow hall. That is my hope, anyway.

So let us take a closer look, then, at the life and death of Richard Alvin Ausley. Let us begin with a great turning point in his life, the almost unimaginably horrible crime he committed against Paul Martin Andrews. The line that connects that crime to Ausley's own murder is a fairly direct one, after all.

At the prison where I met him, there is an entire building full of men like Ausley: rapists and pedophiles within two years of their mandatory release. These prisoners are participants in an innovative sex offender residential treatment program called SORT, which provides intensive therapy to prepare them for their return to society. In my view, SORT is one of the best things the Virginia Department of Corrections does, and I only wish it would be expanded.

Sex offenders form one of the largest subgroups of criminals in prison, and I myself have had several of these men as cellmates over the years. Locked in a seven-by-twelve foot concrete box with the Ausleys of this world, I have learned to distinguish some character traits they have in common. Rapists, for instance, tend to be angry and insecure, while pedophiles show a marked inclination to be timid, fearful, and dishonest.

Anyone familiar with the psychology of sexual abuse *victims* will immediately recognize that second cluster of personality traits: children who are molested frequently try to keep their abusers at bay with exaggerated cautiousness, complaisance, and deception. Why do incarcerated molesters display the same characteristics as their victims? Because the majority of pedophiles in prison were themselves sexually or physically mistreated in their youths.

No, I am not about to revisit "the abuse excuse," as Alan Dershowitz called this phenomenon with inexcusable callousness. But can we really ignore the fact that victims of child abuse are 38 percent more likely to be arrested for a violent crime later in life, with the result that 16.1 percent of male prison inmates admit to having been maltreated as they were growing up?[5]

The actual figure is undoubtedly much higher, since many prisoners do not even recognize that they have been abused. When my fellow inmates recall their childhoods, for instance, they brag of leather belt "whoopings" inflicted by their parents and other horrors. I have actually overheard a rec yard conversation between two sex offenders from the SORT program in which the two prisoners competed with each other as to which one had been molested more horrifically as a boy — as if this were a point of honor between them! Other convicts have told me of growing up in detention centers for troubled youths, where older teens raped younger ones on a nightly basis. In their eyes, this was normal, unremarkable, a suitable subject for joking while we had dinner together in prison years later.

Whether Ausley himself was abused as a child is something I do not know. But it strikes me as exceedingly unlikely that a person brought up in a stable, loving family environment would wake up one day and, out of the blue, start sexually abusing young boys.

Whatever secrets Ausley's childhood might have held, the court did not care when it sentenced him to forty-eight years behind bars in 1973. He was a monster, pure and simple. But once Ausley entered the prison world, the monster became a victim.

As we saw in chapters 2 and 6, inmate-on-inmate sexual assaults are common in U.S. jails and prisons. Child molesters are probably the favorite prey of penitentiary predators, because many guards will not help them if they seek protection. One of the sad ironies of prison "culture" is that incarcerated pedophiles are frequently subjected to yet more of the same sexual violence that they experienced in their youths. In the eyes of other prisoners, garden-variety rapists are not so bad and can be tolerated. But molesters like Ausley are beyond the pale and thus fair game for rape.

From what other convicts who did time with Ausley in the 1970s and 1980s tell me, he had a very rough life indeed behind bars.

Any young or physically small inmate, like Ausley, was subject to sexual enslavement by a "prison daddy" in those days, just like today. While those forced relationships eventually assume a pseudo-consensual nature, however, Ausley was intentionally punished by his fellow prisoners and, by extension, the correctional officers who allowed him to be raped. They wanted to hurt him, and they did — on a monthly basis, for decades, according to my sources.

As an experienced convict, Ausley was occasionally able to deflect onto others some of the aggression directed at him — by pimping out younger, inexperienced prisoners, for instance. And at Mecklenburg Correctional Center in the early 1980s, he managed to pay a gang of young white convicts to protect him. He earned his protection money by selling acrylic paintings, which he produced at an astonishing rate and sent to a gallery in Roanoke, Virginia. Apparently, the gallery's owners did not realize who was supplying them with artwork and ended up befriending Ausley. Even from his penitentiary cell, the aging child molester was able to weave some of his manipulative magic.

By the turn of the century, he was transferred to the low-medium-security prison where I met him: Brunswick Correctional Center, with its SORT program. Even here, however, Ausley could not completely escape his horrific past: "Inmates frown on this type of thing," he told the Richmond *Times-Dispatch* in a jailhouse interview. "There's not a day goes by that I don't hear something — whispers, finger-pointing."[6]

SORT program participants are all subject to at least some low-level harassment by other prisoners. But a few inmates remembered Ausley's original crime and confronted him about it. After his death, another convict came to me and told me had spoken to Ausley as soon as he arrived at Brunswick. "You were my bogeyman as I was growing up," this man said to Ausley. "I grew up near where you lived. When my mom wanted us kids to come inside from the back yard, she would tell us, 'Ausley's escaped from jail, boys, you'd better come indoors.' I grew up *hating* you, man."

Ausley listened and just walked away, according to the prisoner who related this incident to me. No doubt the old child molester had heard it all before.

By sending Ausley to Brunswick, the Department of Corrections presumably intended to prepare him for his return to society by providing him psychosocial therapy. That plan, as far as I am concerned, was both appropriate and intelligent. According to the Bureau of Justice Statistics, the recidivism rate for released inmates fifty-five years old and over is 1.4 percent, and Ausley was now in his early sixties.[7]

Contrary to popular myth, moreover, rapists and molesters are not completely incorrigible: only 17.3 percent commit new sex crimes if they leave prison even *without* receiving treatment during their incarceration. If they *are* given therapy, as was the plan for Ausley, that rate of sexual reoffending can be cut to 9.9 percent, according to a major recent meta-analysis of therapeutic programs conducted by Canada's Solicitor General.[8] And in the three years that Brunswick Correctional Center's SORT program has been in operation, not a single graduate has committed a new sex crime.[9]

Those generally hopeful statistics are somewhat skewed by the fact that roughly 80 percent of sex offenders are of the first-time or familial type, which responds well to treatment efforts.[10] Whether therapy has any effect at all on recidivist pedophiles like Ausley is very much in dispute. Still, the effort had to be made, since his mandatory release date was fast approaching.

In 2002, then, things were looking up for Ausley. He had spent roughly two years in the SORT program and was scheduled for release the following year. But, unbeknownst to Ausley, Paul Andrews had heard of his pending departure from prison and was embarking on a highly public crusade to have him civilly committed.

Richard Ausley had been a known child molester at Brunswick but not a particularly famous one. All this changed in 2002, when Paul

Andrews revisited the nightmarish circumstances of his crime in regular interviews with print and TV journalists. The old pedophile's picture was plastered on the front pages of this state's newspapers at regular intervals. Many inmates read the latest Ausley articles with the same fervent interest as *Sports Illustrated.*

As his fellow prisoners worked themselves into a fury over the details of Ausley's crime — here at last was someone even a convicted criminal could look down upon! — the penitentiary hyenas moved in to exploit his weakness. One well-known snitch offered Ausley his "friendship" if the old man submitted to oral sex. Not that this fellatio would be free of charge: Ausley would have to pay $50 for this dubious "pleasure"! I happened to learn of this particular incident because Ausley refused, whereupon the snitch made good on his threat to get the aging child molester into trouble with the prison administration.

But other inmates were the least of Ausley's trouble. On the other side of the razor wire fence, Paul Andrews, his victim, succeeded in making Ausley the poster boy for civil commitment in Virginia. A fairly recent legal innovation, civil commitment provides for the detention of sex offenders in secure psychiatric facilities even after they complete their formal terms of incarceration. Nineteen states now use this procedure to keep nearly twenty-five hundred rapists and molesters behind bars indefinitely. Fewer than one hundred civilly committed offenders have ever been released, because detainees must first prove to a panel of mental health experts that they no longer pose a threat to public safety.[11]

From Andrews's point of view, this campaign was justified, and I personally sympathize with him. Once again: I am no friend of child molesters. And if ever there was a sex offender who had proved that he could not be trusted again, surely it was Richard Alvin Ausley. He never took responsibility for his many crimes and in a 2003 TV interview even blamed Andrews, his victim.[12]

But there is an old adage in the legal community that runs, "Hard cases make bad law," and it applies well not only to Ausley's but any other sex offender's civil commitment.

After a pedophile or rapist has completed his entire prison sentence, he is in effect put on trial again on the same charges that put him behind bars in the first place. The state calls a series of highly credentialed psychiatrists to testify that this particular sex offender cannot be safely released, and he must somehow prove that they are all wrong. If he fails that judicial test, he is sent to a facility that is a prison in all but name.

The government sidesteps these legal difficulties by pointing out that a trial is a *criminal* proceeding, whereas a commitment hearing is a *civil* cause-of-action. However, that argument does not pass the smell test: both trials and commitment hearings are held in courtrooms, and in both cases the defendant ends up locked in a cell. To nonlegal eyes, there is no real difference.

What civil commitment really does is to absolve society from figuring out how to reintegrate men like Ausley upon their release. In California, the Department of Corrections recently tried to release a civilly committed sexual predator, Cary Verse, who had been chemically castrated and was now considered nondangerous. The residents of Martinez, a town in the northern part of the state, organized opposition to his relocation in their community, forcing him to live in a motel in San Jose instead.[13] That can hardly be considered a case of successful reintegration into society.

Another California sex offender who had completed his sentence, Brian DeVries, had to be housed in a trailer on prison grounds because no town was willing to accept him. And this, in a way, is what civil commitment provides: safe and final disposal of human beings whom no one wants and everyone feels justified in hating.

Virginia provides for civil commitment through its "violent sexual predator" statute of 1999, but the state's General Assembly had never provided funding to construct a facility in this state to house men like Ausley. That changed in 2003, when Andrews succeeded in overcoming the General Assembly's legendary tightfistedness: legislators finally agreed to build the state's first civil commitment unit, the Center for Behavioral Rehabilitation in Dinwiddie County.

Even after the state had guaranteed that Ausley would never see the light of day, the public continued to revile him. When Virginia completed Ausley's very own lockup, the state's largest newspaper vented its righteous anger with the headline "Predators Get Amenities" — because the residents of the thirty-six-bed Center for Behavioral Rehabilitation would be allowed to play basketball and watch TV, just as in a normal penitentiary.[14]

No one saw fit to comment on the unusual design of this facility, however: instead of being housed in cells with walls and solid doors, like in the prisons where they spent the last few decades, the civilly committed offenders were now to be kept in chicken wire kennels erected inside the building. Perhaps there is some therapeutic purpose to this novel architectural arrangement. Perhaps not.

Even though the Center for Behavioral Rehabilitation was built just for him, Richard Ausley did not turn out to be the first resident of this secure psychiatric unit. Paul Andrews had uncovered something else about Ausley's past that made civil commitment unnecessary.

While funding for the special mental health unit to hold Ausley still seemed uncertain, Andrews had tracked down Gary E. Founds of Portsmouth. In 1972, Founds had also been sexually assaulted by Ausley. Andrews persuaded him to break three decades of silence about the crime and testify against Ausley.[15] The resulting conviction and new five-year prison sentence meant that Ausley could be housed in a regular penitentiary for now. So some other sex offender inaugurated the civil commitment facility built for him.

But instead of remaining at Brunswick and continuing in the SORT program, Ausley was transferred to Sussex I State Prison, a facility specifically designed to house disruptive inmates. Just as puzzling as the therapeutic purpose of those chicken wire cages is the therapeutic purpose of Ausley's transfer to Sussex I, where there are no psychologists who work intensively with molesters and rapists.

Department of Corrections spokesperson Larry Traylor told the *Virginian Pilot* that Ausley was relocated to Sussex I because "the latest conviction made it necessary to upgrade his security level."[16] That, however, seems unlikely. Inmate security level classifications are a matter of administrative convenience. For sex offenders enrolled in the SORT program, like Ausley, the security level classifications do not apply at all: there are several SORT participants at Brunswick Correctional Center who were granted security level "overrides" so that they can continue to receive therapy here. Whatever the reason for Ausley's transfer was, his security level was not it.

Among the other prisoners at Brunswick, the most popular theory is that he was moved to Sussex I because he was about to escape again, as he did for six days in the 1970s.[17] But that cannot be the reason either. Even if he had been physically able to break out, years of abuse by other inmates had destroyed Ausley's mind. My general impression of him was that he would have had trouble finding the door, much less escaping through it.

Perhaps the reason for Ausley's transfer is simply that the Department of Corrections decided not to waste expensive SORT therapy on a man who would obviously never be released. There is, in fact, a waiting list for the SORT program, and this old no-hoper was uselessly taking up a slot that another sex offender needed. Perhaps Sussex I was just the nearest prison with an open bed, and Ausley was "turfed" there for convenience's sake.

If that was indeed how his transfer was decided, correctional administrators could hardly have chosen a worse new home for Ausley than Sussex I State Prison. This facility's security classification is 5, just one step below level 6 "supermax," and its inmate population consists of young thugs who act out violently even behind bars. In a Department of Corrections study on rising prison violence entitled "Quarterly Trend Reports, Issue I" — briefly released on the Internet in the summer of 2003 and then quickly removed — Sussex I featured among the leaders for inmate-on-inmate assaults.[18] A wizened, small, extremely well known child molester in his mid-sixties should perhaps have been sent to the geriatric unit at Deerfield Correctional Center — but Sussex I?

Even worse, that facility's administration then placed Richard Ausley into a cell with Dewey Venable. This twenty-four-year-old inmate, who had been sentenced to eighteen years in prison in 2001 for a series of charges that included carjacking, abduction, and robbery, had himself been victimized in 1988 by a pedophile called Dennis S. Sewell.[19] "When prison officials put a person molested as a child in a cell with a child molester, they lit the fuse to a bomb,"

Kent Willis, director of the Virginia chapter of the American Civil Liberties Union, told the *Richmond Times-Dispatch*.[20]

The bomb exploded on January 13, 2004, when Venable strangled and beat Ausley to death. After the murder, Dewey Venable wrote a letter to the *Times-Dispatch* in which he claimed he had warned guards not to place him in a cell with the infamous child molester. According to Venable, however, correctional officers threatened to put him in isolation unless he agreed to the cell assignment. He also claimed to "here [*sic*] voices and see shattos [*sic*]" and has apparently attempted to kill himself.[21]

When informed of Ausley's death, Paul Andrews told the *Times-Dispatch,* "While I cannot condone what happened to him, I certainly can feel for the young man that is being charged with his death. . . . The implications of being abused go far beyond the act of abuse. This young man is another example of the path of destruction left in the wake of a sexual predator, and another life ruined by an encounter with Richard Ausley."[22]

In May of 2004, Venable was indicted in Sussex County, Virginia, for the January 13, 2004, murder by strangulation of Richard Ausley. If convicted under the current indictment, Venable faces the death penalty.[23] And in June, Virginia Secretary of Public Safety John W. Marshall ordered the State Police to conduct an independent review of the Department of Corrections' actions in this matter.[24]

Marshall undoubtedly fears that Ausley's murder behind bars will turn out to be a repeat of the John Geoghan case in Massachusetts. A Catholic priest convicted of child molestation, Geoghan was sent to the high-security unit at Souza-Baranowski Correctional Center, where he was killed in August of 2003 by a fellow inmate, Joseph Druce, who had also been a victim of sexual abuse as a child. "Prison guards harassed pedophile priest John Geoghan and wrote trumped-up disciplinary reports [that] led to the frail, sixty-eight-year-old Geoghan being sent to the high security unit" where he was murdered, Massachusetts Public Safety Secretary Edward Flynn's investigation revealed. "Under no circumstances should John Geoghan have been in the special unit at Souza-Baranowski" prison, Flynn told the Associated Press.[25]

If Virginia Public Safety Secretary Marshall's State Police investigation reaches a similar conclusion in Richard Ausley's killing, then some heads other than Ausley's may end up rolling in this state. The Virginia Department of Corrections is not waiting for Marshall's investigation, however: as of August, inmates arriving at a new prison are no longer placed in any available open bed but are housed in the facility's segregation unit. There they are evaluated by a four-member panel, which includes senior security staff and the institution's psychologist, to determine the new arrivals' compatibility with potential cellmates.

As a convict, I am naturally loath to compliment the Department of Corrections on anything. But I believe that if this new procedure is implemented sensibly — with "sensibly" being the key qualifier — it could revolutionize prison life for the better. What a delicious irony that would be: Ausley the monster might end up being a major force for good in the lives of thirty-one thousand Virginia prisoners.

For the inmates he left behind here at Brunswick Correctional Center, Ausley's needless death has been an eye-opening experience, a "teachable moment." Prisoners who until now missed no opportunity to make snide remarks to sex offenders have suddenly discovered the joys of convict solidarity. Now they shout at passing SORT staff members, "Hope you're proud you got Peewee killed, you @#$%*&!" All of a sudden Ausley is "Peewee," one of us. Who would have predicted that?

But there is a reason that Ausley's story became our own. Back in the real world, the civil commitment movement launched by Ausley's case is gathering momentum. Attorney General Jerry Kilgore's office has already filed twenty-one petitions for civilly committing other sex offenders, two of which have been granted. The thirty-six-bed Center for Behavioral Rehabilitation has been moved and expanded to 150 beds,[26] and plans are afoot to enlarge it again to hold 250 predators.[27] Within a few years, there will be an entire new system of prisons — pardon me, civil psychiatric detention centers — for all sex offenders, since none of them can ever be trusted completely.

Eventually civil commitment will be expanded to crimes that are not of a sexual nature but are also considered especially egregious: homicides and malicious woundings, of course, but perhaps also carjackings and abductions — precisely the kinds of crimes for which Dewey Venable was sent to prison in 2001, three years before killing Richard Ausley. Given the propensity for violence that Venable has displayed even behind bars, a stay at the Center for Behavioral Rehabilitation certainly seems appropriate.

But why stop there? Unless a marijuana dealer can *prove* to a panel of state-paid psychiatrists that he will never sell a single joint again, perhaps he should be civilly committed too. Better safe than sorry!

This sort of thinking has, unfortunately, shaped criminal justice policies in the United States for the last thirty years. At the end of the day, society just wants the evil bastards *gone,* no matter what the cost.

Perhaps this was the kind of emotion that Venable felt when he strangled the old child molester. That young man did not have the option to make Ausley disappear in a civil commitment facility constructed to look like a chicken wire dog kennel, so he throttled him instead. He just wanted the evil bastard *gone,* no matter what the cost.

And who can blame him?

Unfortunately, this understandable human urge to distance ourselves emotionally and in every other way from someone like Ausley can have dangerous consequences, as Christ made clear in the judgment of the nations:

> Then [the King] will say to those on his left, . . . "I was sick and in prison and you did not look after me." Then they also will answer, "Lord, when did we see you . . . sick or in prison and did not help you?" He will reply, "I tell you the truth, whatever

you did not do for one of the least of these [brothers of mine],
you did not do for me." (Matthew 25:41, 43–45, 40)

Ausley was definitely "sick" and definitely "in prison," and if he
was not also "the least," then I do not know who else might be
even less. So precisely who was Jesus talking about in this passage,
if not this frail, old, murdered child molester?

Of course we can try to wriggle out of that question's awkward
answer by denying that Ausley is Christ's brother: after all, only
"to those who believed in his name" does Jesus give "the right to
become children of God" (John 1:12). But how can we be so sure
that Ausley was not granted "the Spirit of sonship [by whom] we
cry Abba, Father" (Romans 8:15)? I lived in the same prison as
he did, and I personally saw him go to Christian church services.
Should we assume he was a pretender?

Still, let us assume for a moment that Ausley *was* faking his
faith: how many true conversions had their start in a church's soup
kitchen, where lost souls came to look for nothing more than a
warm meal and instead found "the living bread that came down
from heaven" (John 6:51)? In a slightly different context, Paul
wrote, "What does it matter? The important thing is that in every
way, *whether from false motives or true*, Christ is preached" (Philippians 1:18). Perhaps, equally, "the important thing is, whether from
false motives or true," the small seed of faith was planted in Ausley's
heart in a penitentiary chapel.

Certainly God's firstborn Son wants "*everyone* to come to repentance," including pedophiles (2 Peter 3:9). "It is not the will of your
heavenly Father that one of these little ones be lost," Christ said to
his disciples, referring to lost sheep (Matthew 18:14). So long as sinners accept him as their older brother, "Jesus is not ashamed to call
them brothers" either (Hebrews 2:11; see also Matthew 10:32–33).
It is, unfortunately, *we* who are ashamed to call Ausley our brother.

To me, this is the very heart of the Gospel: not loving our friends
but our *enemies* (Matthew 5:44). Recognizing child molesters as
"the least of [Christ's] brothers," if they accept him in their hearts.
Not only seeing Richard Alvin Ausley as a brother of ours, but—

heaven help us! — *loving* him. "If you love only those who love you, . . . what are you doing more than others?" (Matthew 5:47, 44).

Christians do not primarily conceive of love as a pleasant emotion, of course, but as practical acts of charity: "Children, let us love not in word of speech but in deed and truth" (1 John 3:18). In the judgment of the nations, for instance, Jesus instructs us very specifically to feed the hungry, welcome strangers, clothe the naked, visit the ill and . . . oh, my goodness, he told us to visit prisoners, too! Surely he could not have meant actually *visiting* someone like *Richard Alvin Ausley,* could he?

Could Christ really, truly have wanted you to join Prison Fellowship Ministries' pen pal program? Was the Son of God really, truly suggesting that you should exchange letters with a convict until you felt you had come to know him or her a little? Was our Messiah really, truly telling you to then drive to a penitentiary, let yourself be patted down by correctional officers, and walk into a visiting room? Did Jesus really, truly intend for you to get some sodas and snacks from the vending machine, and to sit down at the same table with . . . his younger brother or sister?

Is *that* what he meant? Oh, my goodness!

Questions for Reflection and Discussion

1. Traditionally, the prisoners in the judgment of the nations have been interpreted to be Christian missionaries incarcerated for spreading the Gospel — a reading which, if true, would relieve us of the obligation to consider Richard Alvin Ausley as a "brother." In my first book, however, I argued:

   The prisoners Christ speaks of in this passage are in fact one of several different groups of people distinguished, not by their apostolic activity, but by their misfortune. The hungry are not starving themselves *for Jesus,* those without clothes did not become nudists *for the Messiah,* and the sick are not running a fever because they are suffering *for Christ* but simply because they are in need. So there is no justification for limiting our charity for the last group, prisoners, only to those who are behind bars *for their faith*.[28]

While that little paean to universal charity sounds pleasant enough, it is fair to question whether this is really what Jesus intended. Elsewhere Christ warns us not to "throw your pearls before swine," clearly suggesting that not everyone deserves his spiritual gifts — never mind food, shelter, clothing, etc. (Matthew 7:6). Before the emergence of the welfare state, charity was reserved for the so-called "deserving poor." Was this a wiser approach? If yes, would someone like Ausley ever qualify as "deserving"? Why or why not — and if yes, how?

2. Civil commitment is obviously necessary for some offenders. But reflect on the nature of government bureaucracies in this context, as suggested in this chapter. If one builds a civil commitment center for thirty-six men, that is how many violent sexual predators will be found in the prisons of Virginia, for instance. If the facility expands to 150 beds, however, correctional psychiatrists will inevitably find an additional 114 predators to fill those extra beds — men who might not have been determined to be predators when only thirty-six places were available. How does one resolve this conundrum in practice?

3. In this chapter, we learned about two sex offenders whom the state of California recently tried to release — with only very limited success, if any. How would you have felt if Richard Ausley had successfully completed the SORT therapy program and had then moved into an apartment near you? What should be done with men (and a few women) like him?

NINE

The Paraclete

Rough Justice in the Courts

AT THE LAST SUPPER as described in the Gospel of John, Jesus Christ called the Holy Spirit our Paraclete (John 14:16). English Bibles render this term variously as Counselor, Comforter, or Advocate, but in the original Greek the word *parakleitos* simply meant a defense lawyer who spoke for the accused against a *satanos,* or adversary. What a strange thought — of all the metaphors our Messiah could have chosen to explain the Holy Spirit's purpose, Jesus thought it best to describe him as a ghostly Johnnie Cochran, an unearthly F. Lee Bailey, an angelic Alan Dershowitz!

But, on reflection, perhaps this characterization of the third person of the Trinity is not so peculiar after all. By comparing the Spirit to a defense lawyer, Christ extended only slightly an Old Testament figure of speech from the Book of Job. That man of sorrows felt, on the one hand, that Yahweh had put him on trial: "you draw up bitter indictments against me" (Job 13:26). On the other hand, however, he came to see God as his advocate: "I know that my Redeemer lives" (Job 19:25). In ancient Israel, a *ga'al,* or redeemer, was a clan elder who represented his dependents in lawsuits heard at the village gate: an attorney with a personal interest in winning his clients' cases (Ruth 4:1).

When Christ compared the Holy Spirit to a *ga'al* or *parakleitos,* he knew very well that his followers would soon have sore need of legal assistance in particular: opponents of the Way "will hand you over to the courts and scourge you," he warned the disciples (Matthew 10:17). When Jesus promised them a Paraclete to help them at their coming trials, he did not mean a flesh-and-blood attorney, of course, but an interior spirit who "will teach you at that time what you should say" without a trained lawyer's advice (Luke 12:12). And that is awfully convenient for the rest of us in two different ways.

First, since Christians are no longer prosecuted for their beliefs in modern-day America, the third member of the Trinity has really become redundant. "The Bible does not promise us the Holy Spirit's help when we're in court for drunk driving or burglary," a friend told me recently. So we can forget the Paraclete's original function as a real *parakleitos*.

And second, even if some armed robber, say, needs the Holy Spirit's help at trial, we are not responsible for becoming the Spirit's instruments and providing the robber this assistance. Christ said that the Paraclete would come as a supernatural presence *within* the defendant — perhaps leading him to make an apology so heartfelt and sincere that the judge forgives him on the spot. So, again, we can safely ignore the Spirit's role as a courtroom advocate or counselor-at-law.

How convenient — if only it were true!

At the impromptu trial of the woman caught in adultery, Jesus showed us an entirely different side of the Paraclete — as a defender of common criminals who cannot speak for themselves (John 8:1–11). In chapter 3 we saw that Christ did not challenge the law of Leviticus 20:10, which made adultery a capital felony, but instead questioned the authority of the judges: "Let the one among you who is without sin be the first to throw a stone" (John 8:7). This trial tactic is known today as a motion for recusal and, when successful, is decried as one of those awful legal technicalities that lets guilty criminals get off scot-free. Yet our Lord and Savior himself used it to save the life of a felon who, by the law of the land, clearly deserved capital punishment.

Now *either* Jesus was "led by the Spirit" on this occasion as he was at all other times, *or* he was temporarily demon-possessed when he acted as the adulteress's *parakleitos* (Luke 4:1). And if the former is true, then perhaps we should consider whether Christ left us a model to follow here.

There is some urgency to this suggestion because over the last thirty years, America's legal system has become severely dysfunctional. Since church and state are carefully separated in the United States — and perhaps in part also because it is more convenient — Christians are loath to ask, "What would Jesus do?" when it comes to public policy issues like reforming the courts. But the above review of the Holy Spirit's original purpose makes clear that when it comes to legal matters, at least, we really must ask, "What would the *parakleitos* do?"

In the United States, we have an adversarial system of justice that depends on a fair contest between accuser and accused to produce a just result. But because of a rising fear of crime among voters, public officials have tilted the playing field of the courtroom further and further in favor of the prosecution over the last three decades. Small changes to laws protecting the rights of defendants made it easier to win convictions; "truth in sentencing" reforms led to much longer prison terms; and public defender's offices had their budgets and staffs reduced in proportion to district attorney's offices. Through the cumulative effect of such incremental changes, America drifted from being "the land of the free" to being the world's most punitive country.

"Most punitive" surely cannot mean "most Christian," however — not if we believe in a God whose primary attribute is mercy. So it behooves those of us who consider ourselves followers of Jesus to become paracletes, or advocates, for reform of the courts that have washed such tides of humanity into our jails and penitentiaries.

While it is beyond the scope of this book to offer a comprehensive set of proposals to restructure the legal system as a whole, let us examine briefly two areas where changes are necessary and achievable: raising the quality of the *parakleitos* provided to indigent defendants, and moving as many cases as possible to nonadversarial judicial proceedings.

Our courts can produce just results only if the contest between prosecution and defense is fair and even. But in Virginia, to cite one example, court-appointed lawyers are paid just $112 to represent a child in juvenile court, no matter what the crime and no matter how much time the attorney actually has to spend on the case.[1] To defend an adult at a full trial for a felony carrying life in prison, the state pays lawyers no more than $1,096; the average is $245, however.[2] As a result, "attorneys . . . settle cases quickly, even if it is not in a client's best interest," according to a commission studying this issue.[3]

What does a "defense" by an ill-paid and inexperienced court-appointed lawyer look like in real life? Let us look at the case of Sam B., a friend and fellow prisoner of mine at Brunswick Correctional Center in Virginia. Not having a real paraclete cost him his life, as we shall see.

Apart from drunk driving tickets, Sam had no contact with law enforcement until the age of fifty-eight. He spent those halcyon years earning a Purple Heart in Vietnam, working in the advertising industry, and putting his three children through college. Then, unfortunately, Sam killed an intruder inside his own townhouse.

Because he fired two bullets — one more than strictly necessary — Sam was charged with first-degree murder. A reasonably sensible prosecutor offered to let Sam serve nine months in jail in exchange for pleading guilty to manslaughter, but Sam was so convinced of his innocence that he declined this deal. In fact, he even thought it unnecessary to hire a private lawyer and elected to go to trial with a public defender.

This foolhardiness earned Sam a conviction and a twenty-three-year prison sentence. Under the "85 percent/no parole" law in effect in his state, that verdict meant he would have to stay behind bars until he was seventy-eight. But he never made it that far.

In the fall of 2003, at age sixty-three, Sam died from a kidney failure that had initially been misdiagnosed as influenza by penitentiary nurses. Two of his three children were allowed to come to his bedside at the very end, in a prison ward at a local hospital. A correctional officer had to stay in the room, of course — prison rules are prison rules, security comes first! In fact, regulations require that an inmate's corpse must remain handcuffed until a doctor *officially* pronounces him dead.

I took Sam's death very hard and very personally because in our little corner of hell we had become the next best thing to family. Sharing breakfast together, we traded memories of the middle-class lives we were both slowly forgetting and argued over Saddam Hussein's miraculously vanished weapons of mass destruction. We were *friends* in a place where there are supposed to be no human emotions.

But while I am grateful that I had Sam's company for a few years, I am also deeply angry that I met him at all. Sam should never have served more than a year or two in jail, and the only reason he did is that he lacked good legal representation. If a flesh-and-blood *parakleitos* had taken the time to explain the realities of the justice system to him properly, Sam would have accepted that nine-month plea bargain. He was not stupid, just ill-advised.

Of course Sam must carry his share of the blame here: he killed a man, after all. However, the adulteress's guilt did not dissuade Jesus from defending her, either, so I doubt the Son of God would have turned down the chance to represent my friend in court. But on the day of his trial, no one volunteered to become the Paraclete's mouth and arms and legs.

If Sam's story does not persuade you to become involved in improving the quality of public defenders, then perhaps the growing movement toward nonadversarial judicial proceedings may interest you. There are, in fact, other ways of arriving at justice than having a *satanos* and a *parakleitos* do battle.

In so-called drug courts — and, increasingly, mental health courts — minor offenders with substance abuse or psychiatric problems are diverted out of the formal criminal justice process and into treatment programs.[4] Judges work not as imposers-of-punishment but as coordinators of therapeutic services, praising successful participants and holding backsliders accountable at weekly group meetings.[5] In California, this approach lowered recidivism rates by 77 to 85 percent, while Oregon reports savings of $2.50 for every $1.00 spent on drug courts.[6]

From Australia and New Zealand, an even more innovative form of judicial proceedings is now reaching the shores of America: "reintegrative shaming," based on Aboriginal and Maori practices. Victims and offenders who agree to waive formal adversarial trials confer with a trained mediator, supporters from both "sides," and a representative of the local community. At these emotionally intense sessions, criminals face not an anonymous judge behind a bench, but the actual people they harmed, thus forcing offenders to confront and acknowledge the pain they caused. The underlying message of these meetings is: you are still a member of the group, but you need to make drastic changes! The entire New Zealand juvenile justice system was reorganized along these lines in 1989, resulting in significantly lower recidivism rates.[7]

In Maryland, a friend of mine, Mary E., is now working part-time as one of the first volunteer facilitators of such "community conferences," as these sessions are called in the United States. Her job is to help all the participants determine *together* "what restitution the offenders must comply with to repair the harm for which they are responsible," according to researchers led by John Braithwaite of the Australian National University.[8] Mary reports that she is almost always successful in reaching agreements that, on the one hand, bring real healing to victims and, on the other, inspire a sincere determination to restore and reform in offenders.

From a Christian perspective, one might say that Mary's "reintegrative shaming" conferences put into action St. Paul's approach to dealing with a disruptive church member: "Take special note of him. Do not associate with him, in order that he may feel ashamed. Yet do not regard him as an enemy, but warn him as a brother" (2 Thessalonians 3:14–15).

Or one might say that Mary has found a way to do the Paraclete's work, in the precise place where he first made his appearance: the courts of law. Now *that* is what I would call "that old time religion"! But Mary is getting on in years and could probably use a little help. Perhaps, if you listen very closely, you might hear the Spirit calling you?

> Open your mouth in behalf of the dumb
> and for the rights of the destitute.
> Open your mouth, decree what is just,
> defend the needy and the poor!
> (Proverbs 31:8–9)

Questions for Reflection and Discussion

1. In the first paragraph of this chapter, we saw that the New Testament Greek for a courtroom accuser, or prosecutor, is *satanos*. Do you feel shocked and perhaps even offended to find a linguistic link between prosecutors and Satan in the Bible? Why does our society — as opposed to Palestine two thousand years ago — value prosecutors so highly, while making defense lawyers the butts of public ridicule?

2. In 2003 the Center for Public Integrity, a nonpartisan investigative journalism organization in Washington, DC, issued a major study which found that

   > local prosecutors in many of the 2,341 jurisdictions across the nation have stretched, bent or broken rules to win convictions. Since 1970, . . . appellate court panels cited prosecutorial misconduct as a factor when dismissing charges, reversing convictions or reducing sentences in over 2,000 cases. . . . In thousands more, judges labeled prosecutorial misconduct inappropriate, but upheld convictions using a doctrine called "harmless error."[9]

   How do you think you could support reform efforts in this area, in addition to the two areas cited in this chapter?

3. Imagine attending a "reintegrative shaming" session with someone who had committed a crime against you. What would you want to tell the offender? Now imagine that you are the criminal at this meeting and must find words to say to your victim. Could you speak?

TEN

The Legionnaires in the Praetorium

America's Abu Ghraibs

✠✠✠

I N MAY 2004, the United States took a look into the heart of its
own darkness. Young U.S. Army privates and corporals, as American as apple pie, not only sexually tormented Iraqi prisoners of war
in Baghdad's Abu Ghraib prison, but photographed each other in
gleeful poses with their victims. In one unforgettable image, twenty-
one-year-old Pfc. Lynndie England smiled at a masked, blindfolded
man on his hands and knees. And the only excuse she and the others
gave was that they were only following orders — that obscene and
pathetic self-justification of the Nazis convicted at Nuremburg.

What no one has commented on in connection with this sad
tale is the striking parallel to the crucifixion of Jesus Christ. Like
Iraq today, Palestine in AD 33 was a small, Middle Eastern country
under military occupation by an expanding empire's army. Jerusalem's Praetorium, just like Baghdad's Green Zone, was garrisoned
by young soldiers whose main job was to suppress revolutionaries like Barabbas, who "had taken part in a rebellion" much like
Abu al-Zarkawi, the leader of the Iraqi insurgency (John 18:40).
And when the Roman legionnaires laid their hands on one of these
terrorists, they "mocked him" in an all-too-familiar manner: "they
stripped him and put a scarlet robe on him, and then twisted together a crown of thorns and set it on his head" and "struck him on

the head with a staff and spit on him" (Matthew 27:28–29; Mark 15:19). Note that detail: "they *stripped* him" (Matthew 27:28). All that was missing here was the digital camera of Spc. Jeremy Sivits.

In contrast to the Roman soldiers at the crucifixion of Jesus, however, the members of the 372nd Military Police Company at Abu Ghraib were punished for the abuses they committed. And there begins what is perhaps the most disheartening part of this sorry story: the insistent assertion that we are different, we are better.

Before U.S. Army investigators had even completed their reports, President George W. Bush announced that responsibility for the mistreatment of prisoners lay with "a relative few [who] do not reflect the nature of the men and women who serve our country."[1] How convenient! By blaming the proverbial few bad apples — and putting them on public trial with astonishing speed — U.S. leaders managed to turn this scandal into yet another opportunity to perpetuate the myth of America's moral superiority.

It is precisely this myth, this mistaken belief in the unique goodness of the United States, that leads this nation into foolhardy and deadly adventures like the second Iraq war in the first place. In truth, "there is no one righteous, not even one, . . . for all have sinned and fall short of the glory of God" (Romans 3:10, 23). "If we claim to be without sin, we deceive ourselves and the truth is not in us" (1 John 1:8). Only by internalizing and fully accepting this fundamental insight can we hope to avoid more and more Abu Ghraibs in the years and centuries to come.

In the growing public discussion of whether the Iraqi prisoner abuse scandal has any relevance to jails and penitentiaries in America, we find the same dynamic of denial at work again. Staff Sgt. Ivan "Chip" Frederick II and Spc. Charles Graner were employed as prison guards in Virginia and Pennsylvania, respectively. Quite understandably, their families, friends, and co-workers defended them, claiming of each man that "he has never mistreated inmates. . . . He follows the rules and the inmates respect him."[2] This, even though Graner was cited for physical abuse of prisoners in not one but two federal lawsuits.[3] What is more troubling is that prison administrators steadfastly refuse to acknowledge that these two men's actions at Abu Ghraib reflect on the poor quality of the training and supervision they received as guards here in America, and the implications this has for U.S. correctional departments generally.

"Look, there's abuses in school systems, there's abuses in the Catholic Church," said James Gondles, executive director of the American Correctional Association. "In the past twenty years, there's been a sea change in American corrections."[4] Ronald Angelone, the former director of the Virginia Department of Corrections, announced that "there's not a prison system in the United States that teaches anything like that."[5] How convenient, once again: we are different, we are better.

Not all prison administrators are so self-deluding. Chase Riveland, a former secretary of corrections in both Washington State and Colorado, says that "in some jurisdictions in the United States, there is a prison culture that tolerates violence, and it's been there a long time."[6] In Alabama, for instance, misbehaving inmates were commonly tied to "hitching posts" in the hot sun for hours, until the U.S. Supreme Court finally ended this practice in 2002. But the Maricopa County Jail in Phoenix, Arizona, still forces unruly prisoners "to wear women's pink underwear as a form of humiliation," according to the *New York Times*.[7]

My experience of Virginia prisons has persuaded me that leadership is the central factor that determines whether convicts are abused by front-line guards or treated with a minimum of respect and decency. In many, many cases, I have seen unstable and aggressive correctional officers tamed by sergeants who, over time, taught these difficult individuals how to maintain control of their prisoners without overreacting. Unfortunately, I have also seen correctional administrators set conditions in which average officers were allowed to give in to their basest instincts.

In the summer of 1999, for instance, I was transferred to Wallens Ridge State Prison, the second of Virginia's two brand-new "supermax" facilities. I was one of a group of medium-security inmates sent there so that the recently hired guards could practice their "supermax" techniques safely before the real monsters arrived. And my eleven months at Wallens Ridge turned into hell on earth.

Below, I will not distract you with descriptions of beatings and other "regular" abuses. All I will speak of here are those incidents of mistreatment which had some sort of sexual component, since this is what distinguished the photographic excesses of Abu Ghraib.

- As our van rolled into the loading dock at Wallens Ridge State Prison, we were greeted by a phalanx of guards with a German shepherd who sported an erection. Disapproving officers told me later that the canine team manually stimulated their dog in order to send newcomers the message, "We have a hard-on for you."

- Instead of letting us exit the van under our own power in our handcuffs, waist chains, and leg irons, we were literally dragged inside by guards in helmets and riot gear. There we were placed individually in a glass cubicle and ordered to strip, squat, and cough — all in front of a dozen officers of both genders. Then, still in the nude, we had to do an odd little dance in a circle, ostensibly to shake loose any contraband we might have hidden on our bodies.

- Until a federal judge took mercy on us halfway through my stay at Wallens Ridge, none of our shower stalls had curtains — supposedly so that the (frequently female) guards in the day room gun port could shoot us even there (as sometimes happened). During this time, correctional administrators brought visitors into our pod several times, to show off their wonderful new "supermax" facility in operation. I remember distinctly how I myself stood completely naked with shampoo in my hair while visitors of both genders took in the sights.

In view of the frequent shotgun shootings and beatings by guards, the petty harassments (such as being made to kneel and wear leg irons, just to pass through a gate), and the two deaths of inmates that occurred during my eleven months at Wallens Ridge, these incidents of specifically sexual abuse did not seem especially egregious to me and my fellow prisoners at the time. But they are indicative of the tone set by the director of the Virginia DOC at that time, Ron Angelone — the same gentleman who said of Abu Ghraib that "there's not a prison system in the United States that teaches anything like that."

At the opening of Wallens Ridge's sister "supermax," Red Onion State Prison, Mr. Angelone held a speech for new correctional officers and members of the press: "What are [inmates] going to be rehabilitated for? To die gracefully in prison? Let's face it: they're here to die in prison."[8] The guards at Red Onion and Wallens Ridge listened to the intent behind those words, just as the soldiers at Abu Ghraib listened to the intent behind Secretary of Defense Donald Rumsfeld's public ruminations about the inapplicability of the Geneva Convention and the need for "coercive interrogations" of detainees.[9] The result? Naked Iraqi prisoners on a leash and naked Virginian inmates doing odd little dances in glass cubicles.

And two thousand years ago, Roman generals undoubtedly told their legionnaires that the newly conquered province of Palestine needed to be ruled with a very firm hand — nudge nudge, wink wink. The result? A Jewish rabble-rouser whose captors "stripped him" and "mocked him" and "struck him" and "spit on him" (Matthew 27:28–29; Mark 15:19).

Abu Ghraib is Wallens Ridge is Golgotha.

Questions for Reflection and Discussion

1. After Christ's execution, "the centurion who witnessed what had happened glorified God and said, 'This man was innocent beyond a doubt'" (Luke 24:47). This reminds us of Spc. Joseph Darby, the American soldier who exposed the Abu Ghraib prisoner abuses.[10] While all of us like to think that we too would do the right thing in the face of injustice, "the fact is that few people in situations like this actually do resist," says Philip Zimbardo, a Stanford University psychologist. In 1971, he presided over a now-famous experiment in which college students role-played prison guards and quickly became extremely abusive.[11] Moreover, social scientists have been at a loss to explain why some people find the courage to resist when others do evil. One theory is that "they themselves have been scapegoated or turned on by the crowd," according to Dr. John Darley, a professor of psychology and public affairs

at Princeton University.[12] How do you explain the centurion's and Darby's actions?

2. According to James Q. Whitman, a Yale Law School professor specializing in U.S. and European penological practices,

> [t]he American attitude toward degradation in punishment has become dramatically different from that in other countries.... Degradation is regarded as so unacceptable in [European] countries that they have generally barred the use of prison uniforms.... [Inmates] are not housed behind barred doors,... [and] they are not obliged to use toilets in the open view of guards of the opposite sex, as they may be in America.... There are even rules requiring that prisoners be addressed respectfully, as Herr So-and-so.... What has happened in our country? There was a time when America was regarded as a model of civilized punishment.[13]

Reflect on Whitman's question. What are the causes of the wide divergence between European and U.S. attitudes toward degradation in punishment?

3. Were you surprised to read of abuses with a sexual component at Wallens Ridge State Prison, as described in this chapter? Or were you less shocked to find mistreatment of American criminals by correctional officers in "regular" penitentiaries? Do you think that in some way the handling of U.S. convicts can justifiably be rougher than that of foreign prisoners-of-war?

ELEVEN

Simon of Cyrene

Racism in the Courts and in Prison

✠ ✠ ✠

T HE THREE synoptic Gospels begin their descriptions of Christ's crucifixion with an incident whose significance Caucasian-Americans are almost certain to miss. "As [the Roman soldiers] led him away, they seized Simon from Cyrene, who was on his way in from the country, and put the cross on him and made him carry it behind Jesus" (Luke 23:26). Those white readers of the Bible who notice Simon at all are likely to sympathize with him: poor fellow, snatched out of the crowd for no reason, that could have been *me!* But African American Christians know better.

When the Roman soldiers scanned the throng at the Praetorium to find someone to carry Christ's cross, they saw a sea of olive-hued Semitic faces, all more or less alike. The one face that stood out — the one to whom the soldiers assigned the degrading task of carrying a convicted criminal's instrument of execution — was the face of Simon of *Cyrene,* a town located on the northern coast of Africa. Thus his face was most likely darker than those of the native Jerusalemites. Just a coincidence, or an early case of racial profiling?

In the Gospel of Mark, the evangelist identifies Simon as the "father of Alexander and Rufus," who presumably were well-known enough in the early church for his readers to recognize immediately (Mark 15:21). So we can assume that Simon himself had become a Christian and perhaps even one of the "prophets and teachers" at Antioch listed by Luke: "Barnabas, Simon *called Niger,* Lucius of Cyrene, Manaen...and Saul" of Tarsus (Acts 13:1, emphasis added). "Niger" is Latin for "black," indicating that skin color was indeed a characteristic that people in Christ's time noticed. Just as in our own age.

Why bring up the likelihood that the Roman soldiers picked on a black man, called "Niger," to carry Jesus' cross? Because this instance of racism took place in a criminal justice context, the lawful execution of a capital felon. And that should remind all of us of the grossly unequal treatment of blacks by the American criminal justice system today:

- As we saw in chapter 1, this country has an overall incarceration rate of 715 prisoners per 100,000 civilians. Men are incarcerated more frequently than women, and the rate for Caucasian males is actually 990 per 100,000. Black men, however, face odds of 4,834 out of 100,000. Read that again: *4,834 out of 100,000*. By contrast, South Africa caged only 851 black males per 100,000 in the last year of apartheid.

- More than one-fifth of all African American men aged thirty to thirty-four are now, or already have been, locked up, and that number is projected to rise.[1]

- In Washington, DC, the capital of "the land of the free," *half* of all young black men are in jail, on probation, or on parole.[2]

- African American offenders constituted 21 percent of prison admissions in 1926, but 50 percent of prison admissions in 1996.[3]

- While less than 1 percent of white children currently have an incarcerated parent, 7 percent of black boys and girls are growing up with one or both parents behind bars.[4]

Perhaps Simon of Cyrene is not the most elegant way of drawing attention to these extremely troubling facts. But somebody had better start noticing them somewhere, sometime.

In fact, prison administrators like New Jersey Department of Corrections Commissioner Devon Brown are well aware of the racial disparities in U.S. jails and penitentiaries. Fully 63 percent of New Jersey's inmates are African American, for instance, although only 12.3 percent of the civilian population is black.[5] As a result, "there are those who, with some degree of justification, have proclaimed our prisons as being America's new plantations," Commissioner Brown said at Rutgers University in November 2003. "Not since slavery has our country promoted policies which have visited such enormous economic and human calamity on the black community."[6]

To no one's surprise but his own, this bit of truth-telling nearly cost the commissioner his job. A prison guards union, the New Jersey Law Enforcement Supervisors Association, called on the state's governor, James E. McGreevy, to fire their boss for making the "highly inappropriate and racially charged" speech quoted above. In the end, the governor's spokesperson, Ellen Mellody, had to publicly reassure the guards that no one in the governor's office was taking Commissioner Brown's jeremiad seriously.

As a German citizen who has spent approximately the last two decades in Virginia prisons, I have a unique and arguably useful perspective on the role of race in America's court and prison systems. On the one hand, white inmates regard me as something of an outsider because I am a foreigner. Black prisoners, on the other hand, initially regard me as an outsider, too — until they get a chance to learn a bit about me, after which they sometimes accept me as one of their own.

When I first arrived at my current penitentiary, for instance, I landed a job in the recreation department (gym) as the weekend visiting room photographer, taking pictures of convicts with their families. One of my co-workers in the gym was a gentleman named Funk, the biggest, baddest, and blackest weightlifter in the prison. Along with his stickman Mikey ("He'll eat anything"), Funk presided over the weight room, where he kept the rest of us from hitting each other over the head with dumbbells.

Since Funk and Mikey wanted to know all about the new arrival, I told them the sorry tale of a college honors student from Germany who was railroaded in a small country town in Virginia for a double-murder he did not commit. Very few inmates claim they are innocent, contrary to popular myth, so my story often finds interested and occasionally even sympathetic listeners among my fellow convicts. What really grabbed Funk and Mikey is the reasons I gave for *why* the authorities chose to railroad me: they needed to convict someone, anyone, of a gruesome, unsolved crime, and I was an outsider without connections to the local "good ol' boy" network.

It was at this stage in my narration that Funk spoke up: "Boy, they was out to hang your ass from the get-go. Them rednecks couldn't find themselves a black man to string up, so they snatched you. You ain't one a them, you from over the water somewheres. You a nigga just like us."

Whereupon Mikey started cackling like a hyena and rolled around on the floor, as he is wont to do once or twice a day. "You a nigga, you a German nigga," he hollered over and over again. And it must be true, for when I called him and Funk niggas back, they did not beat me to a pulp!

So that is how I got in touch with my inna nigga and personally breached the color barrier in a penitentiary in the Deep South. But as heartwarming as this little incident is, it is far from typical in the racially charged atmosphere of American prisons. The Human Rights Watch report *No Escape: Male Rape in U.S. Prisons,* for instance, found that "white inmates are disproportionately targeted for abuse. . . . Sexually abusing someone of another race or ethnicity, *with the exception of a white inmate,* could lead to racial or ethnic unrest."[7]

Unfortunately, I can confirm Human Rights Watch's findings personally. I escaped being raped, but many Caucasian-American inmates of my acquaintance were not so lucky. In many ways, U.S. prisons have become venues of racial revenge, where underclass blacks vent their anger on whites because here, at last, *they* are in the majority.

Can anything or anyone heal these wounds and bridge these divides? Frankly, I am not hopeful. But there is one figure in our Bible who may point to the beginnings of a solution: Ebed-Melech the Cushite.

During the Babylonian army's siege of Jerusalem in 587 BC, the prophet Jeremiah was incarcerated in the king's cistern for warning that the war was lost. Only one man risked royal displeasure by speaking up for Jeremiah and then personally pulled him out of the cistern: the man from Cush, a city in Ethiopia. Could it be that Ebed-Melech's black skin had earned him some firsthand experience with injustice and thus sensitized him to the prophet's plight?

I believe so. And I believe that one of the lessons white America could learn from Ebed-Melech today is that *Caucasians* are the ones who are imprisoned by the racism in this country's criminal justice system. Through their own prejudices and the immense suffering those prejudices inflicted on the black community — *4,834 out of 100,000!* — whites have placed themselves in the slime at the bottom of a deep cistern of sin. Getting out of that hole will not be as easy as taking charge, "fixing" the problem, and freeing African American prison inmates by the hundreds of thousands.

Instead, Caucasian-Americans must hope that some African American Ebed-Melechs will stretch out their hands of forgiveness and pull them back up to the light of day. Blacks are the ones who have been horribly sinned against here, so they are the ones who have the right to decide that it is time to "move on." Meanwhile, whites might do well to heed Jeremiah's advice in his Lamentations: "Let us search and examine our ways, that we may return to the Lord! Let us reach out our hearts toward God in heaven" (Lamentations 3:40–41).

> When anyone tramples underfoot
>   all the prisoners in the land,
> when he distorts men's rights
>   in the very sight of the Most High,
> when he presses a crooked claim,
>   the Lord does not look on unconcerned.
>   (Lamentations 3:34–36)

Questions for Reflection and Discussion

1. In the letters to the Galatians and the Colossians, Paul addresses racism directly: "Here there is not Greek and Jew,

circumcision and uncircumcision, barbarian, Scythian, slave, free; but Christ is all in all" (Colossians 3:11; see also Galatians 3:28, which also refers to gender discrimination). How do you explain that slavery could continue to be practiced in Christian countries, including the United States, well into the nineteenth century? What justifications used then do we still employ today to avoid ending discrimination?

2. In a recent study of the death penalty, researchers at Cornell University found a complex set of relationships between race and the imposition of capital punishment. For instance, blacks commit 51.5 percent of all murders nationally but constitute only 42 percent of death row inmates, suggesting that African Americans are actually sentenced to death less frequently than whites.

   Race does continue to play a statistically significant role when the victims are Caucasian-Americans, however: blacks who murder whites are sentenced to death 2.5 times as often as whites who murder whites (66 per 1,000 versus 26 per 1,000). And in Virginia, blacks who murdered blacks were sentenced to death 0.4 percent of the time, while blacks who murdered whites were sentenced to death 6.4 percent of the time. The rate for white killers of whites was 1.8 percent; for white killers of blacks, 2.3 percent.[8]

   How do you explain these differing statistical trends? What do you think could be done to overcome the effects of racial discrimination not only in death penalty cases, but in the criminal justice system as a whole? Is it possible to combat racism in the courts and prisons only, or will it be necessary to address larger social issues that contribute to crime: poverty, education, single-parenthood?

3. In the very heart of Berlin, next to the Bundestag (the former Reichstag), my native country of Germany has built an enormous memorial to the victims of the Holocaust, as well as a major museum. Would Caucasian-Americans be more able to confront the evil legacy of slavery if a memorial to

its victims were built on the Mall in Washington, DC? How can the unconscious racism of whites be brought more into consciousness? How can blacks be shown that the depth of their continuing suffering from the historical consequences of slavery is fully recognized by the nation as a whole?

TWELVE

The Good Thief

Correctional Education

✠✠✠

TODAY IS graduation day in the penitentiary, so all the convicts who have earned some sort of degree are lined up outside the back door of the visiting room in their tasseled caps and black gowns. For almost all of them, this is the very first time that they have ever succeeded at anything that society values, so of course they do their best to pretend to each other that the upcoming ceremony means nothing to them. *Gotta be cool, bro!* But strangely enough, there is no horseplay in the line, no arguments about poker debts or football pools. The usual prison controversies seem to have vanished for a while, and these inmates have become — pardon the expression — well behaved.

From inside the visiting room, the opening strains of "Pomp and Circumstance," the graduation march, can now be heard, so the gowned prisoners begin to file in and take their seats in the middle section. To their right sit the facility's academic and vocational teachers and the so-called "teacher's aides," those exceedingly rare inmates whose educational level allows them to assist the civilian staff members in their classroom work. And to the graduates' left is a sadly small section of chairs for their family members. Like last year, less than twenty visitors have showed up for today's ceremony, though nearly one hundred prisoners will receive their diplomas.

The miracle of orderliness that began in the line outside now continues indoors as the convicts sit through a series of mind-numbing speeches by the warden, the prison education department's "principal," and an ex-inmate who has succeeded in "the real world" thanks to the schooling he received right here in "the big house." The only relief in this part of the proceedings comes when the warden thanks the guards for providing "security" for the academic and vocational staff. That always raises some laughs.

After the civilian dignitaries have given their speeches, it is finally one of the convicts' turn: the honor graduate, the man who has made the most progress, though not necessarily the highest grade. His remarks may be less polished, but they are listened to carefully because even the dimmest minds present can understand that the honor graduate represents hope. If *this* jerk can come *that* far even in *here*, then maybe I can keep pushing myself further and get another certificate next year.

Today's honor graduate is Charlie, a man from this facility's special mental health unit. In many ways, he is a typical convict: as we saw in chapter 2, over 400,000 of America's 2.2 million prisoners have been diagnosed with a mental illness so severe that even penitentiary nurses cannot ignore it. Usually these men are mixed in with, and exploited by, other convicts, but this prison houses them in a special separate building. Charlie himself has served nine years of a fifty-year sentence for first-degree murder and can expect to remain behind bars until he is in his late forties. In addition to his mental illness, he is afflicted with a low IQ, another common characteristic of convicts.[1]

But in spite of these obstacles, Charlie has performed a small miracle: within only three years, he progressed from the lowest level of academic classes (remedial reading) all the way to earning his GED (high school equivalency), *and* he passed almost all the requirements of the Introduction to Computers course (except for reaching a typing speed of thirty-five words per minute). *That* is something worth celebrating, even by those inmates who consider themselves smarter and tougher than Charlie. When he finishes speaking, he gets a real round of applause, not the polite clapping bestowed on the warden and the others.

And then, at last, comes the high point of the ceremony: one by one the prisoner-students are called to the podium to receive their certificates. Here comes young Trey, who has been inside since he turned fifteen and will get out next spring at twenty-three; he does the "gangsta" strut on the way to the front, but on the way back he forgets to show off for his friends because he is so absorbed by the gold-lettered diploma. Next is Old Man Wilkins, in his thirty-first year on three life sentences; he has now completed apprenticeship programs in every single vocational trade available, and without him no toilet around here would ever get unplugged, no light bulb replaced, and no lock fixed. When an inmate goes forward who has struggled in his studies, his classmates cheer and whoop, an otherwise unimaginable display of manly affection.

Despite these successes, this graduation day is a profoundly depressing affair on one level because so many of these men had to come here, to the penitentiary, to be infected by the education "bug." Proper schools were simply not available where they lived because tax dollars were diverted from classrooms to cellblocks during the last fifteen to twenty years. Between 1987 and 1998, for instance, correctional budgets grew 30 percent while elementary and high school expenditures dropped 1.2 percent and university spending fell by 18.2 percent.[2] California built twenty-one penitentiaries between 1984 and 1994, but only one university.[3] "Every time you build a prison, you close a school," Victor Hugo noted long ago. And as a result, 43.1 percent of state prisoners have no high school diploma or GED, and 59 percent are either completely or functionally illiterate.[4]

Many black inmates have taken to calling the penitentiary "Nigga U.," as in university — " 'cause the joint is the only place a nigga can get an education in these here United States." But only 23.4 percent of state prisoners actually participate in GED/high school programs, and only 9.9 percent have taken even one community college course behind bars.[5] Why? Because funding has been cut for correctional education, too: in 1982, there were 350 college programs in prisons in the United States, whereas in 2001 there were fewer than 12.[6] Thanks for this policy change must go to President Bill Clinton, whose 1994 decision to deny Pell Grants to inmates inspired most states to eliminate prisoner eligibility for state tuition grants, too.[7]

Yet correctional education has consistently proved to reduce recidivism rates dramatically. Among New York ex-convicts under twenty-one, earning a GED while incarcerated lowered their chances of returning to jail by a full 25.9 percent.[8] And in a 1991 New York study, those inmates who completed a college program behind bars were almost twice as likely not to reoffend as those who began but did not finish their studies.[9]

Anyone seriously interested in reducing crime, as opposed to merely appearing to be "tough on crime," might do well to pay attention to these figures, and to the anecdotal evidence presented by Charlie and the others at this penitentiary's graduation day. Each and every year, 625,000 prisoners are released back into society because their sentences are over; nothing can stop their coming.[10] Really, the only choice America has is whether all those ex-convicts show up *with* an education that will help them get and keep a legal job — or *without* any skills, except drug-dealing and house-breaking.

Or, to use a Christian idiom, does this country want good thieves or bad thieves? Jesus considered this question so important that he devoted the last few minutes of his life to demonstrating the correct answer for us. Consider the alternatives he had as he hung on his cross: he could have pronounced judgment on the Pharisees, or held a grand speech of encouragement for his disciples, or publicly revealed himself as the Son of God. But instead, our Messiah talked quietly with a couple of lousy criminals, two "dirtbags" as Andy Sipowitz would have called them on *NYPD Blue*. And he managed to save at least one of them.

Of course Christ did not conduct a high school equivalency course on the cross, nor did he teach the two thieves plumbing. If anyone is looking for an excuse to reduce correctional education budgets still further, perhaps this is it: Jesus only wants us to save prisoners' souls, not to actually help them become better citizens! What I think Christ tried to show us in his final moments, however, is that even the seemingly most irredeemable characters can turn their lives around, *if* they are given just a little encouragement, a little assistance.

In his letter to the Ephesians, Paul wrote that "the thief must no longer steal, but rather labor, doing honest work with his own hands, so that he may have something to share with one in need" (4:28). This is a verse much used by prison ministers to exhort their incarcerated congregations to change their wicked ways, and it is certainly helpful to remind inmates that they must obey the laws of God and man. In our context here — the importance of correctional education — it is also encouraging to see that the Bible makes allowance for the possibility that thieves can indeed be reformed and earn their living in some legal way.

But those sitting in the pews of penitentiary chapels across America are apt to notice at least two other facets of, or angles to, Ephesians 4:28 that prison ministers somehow often seem to miss. First, we sinners serving time find it remarkable that the church at Ephesus apparently welcomed members who were known to be semi-retired thieves; what congregation in the United States can make *that* claim today? And second, we prison parishioners cannot help but wonder how we are to acquire the means of "doing honest work with [our] hands"; where do we get the skills and then the job opportunities? Preaching to us that we "must no longer steal" would be a much more effective message if it came with some down-to-earth vocational training and job placement assistance.

By taking up the challenge I lay down for you here, you can do the same work that our Messiah did on the cross: you can turn a bad thief into a good one. Remember, even inmates are able to do this, as the "teacher's aides" demonstrate every day in penitentiaries across the country. If a lousy convict, a "dirtbag," is able to imitate Christ by teaching another convict how to read, perhaps, just maybe, you could, too.

Contact your nearest jail or prison and ask how to become a remedial literacy volunteer, how to set up a twelve-step program, how to teach resumé-writing and job-interview techniques. Tell them Jesus sent you!

> I have not come to call the righteous,
> but sinners to repentance....

> There will be more rejoicing in heaven
>   over one sinner who repents
> than over ninety-nine righteous persons
>   who do not need to repent.
>   (Luke 5:32, 15:7)

Questions for Reflection and Discussion

1. Can you imagine doing what Christ did on Golgotha: spending your final moments in conversation with two criminals?
   What would you consider more important, if you knew you
   were about to die? Do you think Jesus should have chosen
   more worthy subjects for his last words — and who should he
   have given preference, instead of prisoners?

2. One of the common objections to rehabilitative programs for
   convicts is that they are money wasted, since 67.5 percent of released inmates are arrested again within three years anyway.[11]
   But according to a recent study by the Legal Action Center, all
   fifty states have "laws that bar former offenders from whole
   professions...unrelated to their crimes,...or strip them of
   driver's licenses, parental rights and the right to vote....This
   country only harms itself when it traps ex-offenders at the
   margins of society and forces them back into prison," the
   New York Times argues.[12] Would it be possible, instead, to
   link educational programs behind bars with specific jobs on
   the outside, so ex-offenders can transition directly from a ma-
   sonry course in prison, say, to a construction company with
   an opening? What could you do to develop such a program?

3. How would you feel if your employer were to hire an ex-
   convict and place him or her at the desk next to yours at the
   office? Would your reaction depend on the former prisoner's
   gender, race, or offense? What crimes would you consider acceptable, and which ones would make you look for another
   job? Do you think you should be told that your new co-worker
   is a released convict, or should he or she have a (perhaps
   limited) right to keep that information private?

THIRTEEN

The Bad Thief

Life Sentences

✠✠✠

T HERE IS A CHIP in the paint on my bunk bed where Keith hung
himself. Like everything else in prison, penitentiary paint is
cheap: even a suicide's shoestring rope is enough to nick it. That
scratch is all that is left of Keith now.

In the year or so that we shared a cell, Keith and I never really
became friends. This is not unusual, however: prison life is not exactly conducive to genuine emotional bonding. To survive behind
bars, you have to be constantly on your guard against the infinite
variety of smiling manipulators. Years can pass before you accept
another man as your "associate" or "stickman" and extend just
a little trust to him. Even then, you never call him your "friend";
in the penitentiary, that term can easily be misunderstood to mean
one's homosexual lover.

So Keith and I lived side by side, or on top of one another, in
our seven-by-twelve-foot concrete box while essentially remaining
strangers. Of course we sometimes passed on prison gossip, discussed politics and shared brief memories of uncontroversial parts
of our pasts. But it was not until after his suicide that I found out
why he had come to the penitentiary in the 1990s: for aggravated
sexual battery on a minor.

What little I did come to know of Keith in our year together, I
liked a lot. He took a shower every day, he always used headphones
while watching his five-inch TV, he did not steal from me, he did

not try to rape me or start a consensual sexual relationship with me, he did not use drugs or brew homemade alcohol, he passed gas and snored within reasonable limits, he kept quiet during my four daily Centering Prayer sessions, and he did not press conversation on me when I did not want it — which I never do. All this made Keith an ideal cellmate for me, a veritable gift from heaven: for all practical purposes, he was invisible, unnoticeable, absent.

Now, of course, he is truly and permanently absent. And I miss him. I really do.

The last time I saw him alive was on April 27, 2004, at 6:10 a.m. Like every morning, I had performed Centering Prayer from 5:00 to 5:30 a.m. and then read my Bible and written a letter. He got up once and urinated while I prayed, and his T-shirt very gently brushed my arm as he passed. Ten minutes after six, as I left the cell to go to breakfast, I saw him stirring on the bottom bunk, as if to rise and follow me. Just like every morning.

We had waffles that day, but I did not see Keith come through the chow line. So I left the dining hall early and returned to our housing unit to wake him up, to let him know that he could still make it to breakfast before the chow line closed if he left immediately. I remember looking at my watch: it was 6:30 a.m. In a rush to ensure that Keith did not miss his waffles, I jerked open our cell door and...

The cell lights were off. Keith appeared to be sitting on the floor with his back against his bottom bunk, and I could see some blood on the front of his white T-shirt. I thought he had lost consciousness because of diabetic shock and then experienced a nosebleed.

According to what other inmates told me later, I shouted, "Oh my God!" I remember running to get the guard from the dayroom and returning with her to the cell. She was the one who turned on the light. And that is when we saw the white rope made of shoestrings, tied to my top bunk railing.

Both of us could see immediately that Keith was definitely and completely dead.

After that, everything went crazy. Other inmates from surrounding cells, alerted by my initial exclamation, crowded around the open door to catch a glimpse of the dead guy. The guard I had brought to the cell was now also shouting "Oh my God" repeatedly, until someone pointed out to her that she really should radio for help. A few minutes later, some male guards arrived with a nurse, cut Keith down, and attempted CPR. They tried very hard — I'll say that for them — but it was too late.

Meanwhile, still other guards had shepherded the other prisoners into their cells and put me in the now-empty dayroom. I watched them carry Keith past me on a stretcher. And then I just sat there for an hour or two.

Next came the inevitable interrogations: the institutional investigator, a senior staff member, an investigator from Department of Corrections headquarters, and finally a whole group that included all of the above, plus a psychologist and a computer expert. "We think you know something you're not telling us," the senior staff member announced ominously; in the penitentiary, this is known as "squeezing my balls." Amazing, how everything in prison has to be someone's fault — even a suicide.

Eventually, everyone appeared to agree that I was just as surprised and shocked as I appeared to be. So I was told that I could leave, and that I should pack up Keith's property.

Of course this was really the responsibility of two guards assigned to this task, but they were too scared to enter "the hangin' cell." With the help of another prisoner, I swept all of Keith's belongings into several enormous black trash bags, so the investigator could rummage through everything later. Everything except Keith's Diet Cokes, that is — the other inmate kept all of those, as well as two bars of soap and a deodorant. Such is penitentiary life.

Perhaps I am no better. My first priority after packing Keith's property was to get a sponge, broom, and mop bucket and remove any trace of him. That cell never got a cleaning as thorough as the one I gave it on the day of his death.

By then it was nighttime. So I took a shower, turned off the cell lights, and climbed into my top bunk. Then I climbed back down, turned the small light on again, and returned to bed. Sleeping alone in that cell with no lights at all was more than even I, with all my penitentiary experience and toughening-up, could stand.

The next morning, someone in authority must have figured out that I should not have been allowed to return to the cell and spend the night there. So I was told to pack up my own belongings and move into another cell for a week. Meanwhile "the hangin' cell" was officially, if belatedly, put "under investigation."

That investigation failed to turn up any evidence of why Keith took his life. According to the institutional investigator, who discussed this matter with the Department of Corrections' chief psychologist, suicides who are truly determined to die neither signal their intentions beforehand nor leave any explanatory letters for afterward. But among inmates and staff, there was plenty of speculation.

The prison's computer class, where Keith had worked as a "teacher's aide," had been the subject of an investigation in the week leading up to his death. Supposedly, computer-generated child pornography had been found on the hard drive, and Keith had killed himself to escape the consequences. Given the nature of the crime that had sent him to the penitentiary originally, the discovery of kiddie porn in his possession could conceivably have led to his civil commitment as a repeat sex offender upon completion of his current prison sentence in 2016.

But one week after the suicide, a senior staff member assured me that child pornography had not in fact been found in the computer class or anywhere else.

Another theory was that Keith had sought admittance to this prison's innovative Sex Offender Residential Treatment (SORT) Program, a nationally recognized success. Under the current correctional regime, however, he would have had to serve another full decade behind bars before he could enter SORT in the last two years prior to his scheduled release. Wanting to change yourself is not enough to earn a second chance — not anymore.

But Keith read newspapers and thus was aware of the political realities affecting prisoners, so he could hardly have been surprised by the mercilessness of the system.

Thus, in the end, all that the few of us who liked Keith are left with is a mystery. He wanted out — a sentiment all of us understand — and he found a way out. What many of the rest of us have been asking ourselves is why we are not following Keith's way of making parole.

No one wants to say this out loud, of course. But I can see it in the slumped shoulders, and I hear it in the joking advice to "keep hangin' in there, buddy." Was Keith a kind of penitentiary prophet, showing us all some ugly truths about our own lives?

In the housing unit where he and I lived, there are many inmates who will most likely die behind bars: lifers who will never be released. There are currently 127,677 prisoners serving life sentences in this country's state and federal penitentiaries, an amazing one in every eleven inmates.[1] In the federal system and six states, lifers are officially ineligible for parole, but even those states whose laws technically still allow the release of such prisoners, actual parole grants are virtually unheard of for those serving life.

Thus the comparatively small penitentiary where I am housed holds at least two men who have spent over forty years behind bars, several with more than thirty under their belts, and literally dozens in the "twenty-plus-years" club. With only eighteen years of incarceration at that time — almost precisely half my life — I am actually considered a "fresh fish" around here.

We lifers, we are the dead. Our executions may be stretched out over four or five decades, but in the end, "life without parole" produces exactly the same result as lethal injection: 127,677 human beings killed by their government.

All of us lifers know this, yet for some reason *we* are not the ones who killed ourselves. Keith, a man who actually had a firm release date — albeit twelve years from now — *he* is the one who committed suicide. Why?

I do not know.

I do know that I wish I had listened to Keith, even to his silence. So much of my life now is spent on Centering Prayer, the prayer of inner silence, that I was grateful to have a taciturn cellmate like Keith. Someone mature enough to keep quiet, watch his TV without bothering me, and let me do my praying and writing. Someone who did not need a babysitter.

So I failed to be my brother's keeper. Admittedly, Keith seems not to have wanted someone to talk him out of hanging himself. But the fact is that I never even tried.

When I turn to my Bible as I struggle with Keith's suicide, I find two passages that shed at least some light on his death: the stories of Samson and the so-called "bad thief."

You will recall that, thanks to Delilah, Samson was finally captured by the Philistines, "bound...with bronze fetters [and] put to grinding in the prison" (Judges 16:21). On one occasion, while being taunted in the great hall by "about three thousand men and women [for their] amusement," he pushed down the columns and "killed at his death...more than he had killed during his lifetime" (Judges 16:30). So scripture tells us, anyway.

But I suspect that biblical truth sometimes is deeper than the obvious literal meaning of the text: as a prisoner myself, I think I can recognize another prisoner's fantasy. There is not an inmate alive who has not dreamed of ending his own pain in a grand final gesture and taking as many of his captors with him to the grave as possible. Whoever wrote the story of Samson's suicide was probably a convict himself, and he expressed a very important and sad truth about life in the penitentiary: hopelessness kills.

I am sure that Keith would have pushed down the columns of the great hall if he could have. But in the end, even this satisfaction was denied him. And that would have only added to his hopelessness.

The other Bible passage that has given me at least a little perspective on Keith's death is the description of the "bad thief" at Jesus' crucifixion. Traditionally, Christians focus on the "good thief," the repentant one, that symbol of mercy in extremis. How heartwarming! But most of America's 127,677 lifers, and almost certainly my cellmate Keith, identify more closely with the "bad thief," the one who died without hope and with curses on his lips (Luke 23:39).

Much like modern-day jailbirds, the "bad thief" had probably learned that central rule of prison life with which I began: do not let anyone get close to you! An occasional "associate" or "stickman" is acceptable — but no "friends," please. Trust no one! Especially not some nutcase on the cross next to yours who claims he is the Son of God.

Yeah, sure, buddy — and I'm the Shah of Iran. Let me do my time, and you do yours. And keep the noise down, will ya!

That is how I lived while sharing a cell with Keith: I failed to recognize him as a child of God. The light eternal, the light that shone before the creation of the universe, this light was flowing through Keith every single day that we were cellmates — and I did not see it. God's beloved son was in the bunk bed below mine, but I was to busy praying and writing to pay attention.

"This is how all will know that you are my disciples: if you love one another," Jesus said at the Last Supper (John 13:35). I was a poor disciple, and I am so sorry. May God have mercy on Keith's soul — and also on mine.

Questions for Reflection and Discussion

1. According to some denominations' statements of faith, grave psychological disturbance or anguish can diminish the responsibility of one committing suicide to the extent that God may pardon this self-murder. Do you feel that the circumstances of Keith's life diminish his responsibility for his act? Why or why not? How about inmates who will never be released? Or death row prisoners?

2. Jesus said, "Whosoever speaks a word against the Son of Man will be forgiven; but whoever speaks against the Holy Spirit will not be forgiven" (Matthew 12:32). The "bad thief" on the cross next to Christ's taunted only him but did not curse the Holy Spirit. Do you think God can provide some opportunity for repentance for the "bad thief," even after death? Why or why not?

3. In the September 1971 Attica prison riot, some modern-day Samsons attempted to do what the Old Testament hero did when he pushed the great hall's columns down. Now that you have read a little about modern-day prison conditions in the

pages of this book, are you surprised there are so few riots today? What might explain this phenomenon?

4. If you were a prison volunteer and had been visiting Keith in some capacity, what words might you have said to give him hope? What would you say to someone who will never be released?

FOURTEEN

The Resurrection

A Convict's New Life

✝✠✝

T HE DIFFERENCE between Keith and me is Jesus. For fourteen
years, from 1986 to 2000, thoughts of suicide — and, indeed,
the means to commit it — stayed with me constantly. I am certain I
would have killed myself in 2001, had Christ not given me new life
by then.

Between 1986 and 1990, while fighting extradition from England
to the United States, I kept a rope and noose made from bed sheets
hidden in my prison mattress, so I could "cheat the hangman" before returning to America on death penalty charges. The European
Court of Human Rights eventually lifted the threat of execution,
but in 1990 a jury in Virginia found me guilty of double murder —
an injustice so intolerable to me that I tied a plastic bag over my
head with a shoelace on the night of that verdict. Throughout the
next decade, I kept two or three hundred aspirin hidden in a Meta-
mucil jar that traveled with me to three different prisons. The time
to take those pills seemed to have arrived in January 2001, when
the U.S. Supreme Court denied my lawyer's final appeal and in effect sentenced me to die of old age in a cage. What was there left to
live for?

A great deal, thanks to Jesus. I had become a Christian in 1994,
but it was not until 2000 — one year before that terrible denial by
the Supreme Court — that I developed a really intense, personal
relationship with our Savior. Through the Reverend Beverly Cosby

(United Church of Christ), I had at last learned how to truly pray, to "be still before the Lord [and] wait for God" (Psalm 37:7; see also 46:11).

From my perspective, the new life granted to the convicted criminal Jens Soering is no less miraculous than the resurrection of the executed felon Jesus of Nazareth. Three prisoners were put to death on Golgotha, but *one* rose from the grave and thereby saved me, another prisoner, from dying physically and spiritually two thousand years later. If that is not a miracle — or, as the evangelist John puts it, a "sign" — then I do not know what is.

My story thus is little more than a retelling of Christ's. In both cases, resurrection turned out to be not just a reward for "good" people in the afterlife, but a reality for two lowly convicts in *this* life, *today*. Indeed, Jesus comes alive again in a special way each time some anonymous prisoner somewhere accepts our Savior into his or her heart.

Unless someone leads that unknown convict to Christ, however, no resurrection behind bars can take place. That is the reason why I want to share with you my faith journey in the following pages: to tell you about the real hero of my story, Bev Cosby. It was through him that Jesus came to me and saved my life and soul. How did this miracle happen? Where did it all start?

I entered the world in Bangkok, Thailand, in 1966 because my father, a West German diplomat, was stationed at our country's embassy there. Since neither of my parents ever attended a Christian church, they introduced their newborn son to organized religion by taking him to the local *wat,* or temple, to be chanted and prayed over by orange-robed monks. But it was not only a Buddhist bug that bit me in the Land of Smiles: just one year later, Father Thomas Merton, the famous monk, mystic, and author of *Seven Storey Mountain* and *Seeds of Contemplation,* died across town in a hotel room, and I like to imagine that his departing soul gave mine a nudge in the right direction before racing home to its Source.

Shortly after that fleeting spiritual encounter, my father was transferred to the West German embassy in Cyprus, the site of Paul's first overseas mission (Acts 13:4–12). Of course I did not realize then that the very same ground I walked on daily had carried the first Christian saints two thousand years earlier; but who is to say that the shores of Paphos left no mark on my childish soul, just as my little feet left prints in its sand? Is that not what we hope for when we go on pilgrimages to the Holy Land?

A few years later, our family moved again, this time to the Foreign Ministry's home office in Bonn, West Germany, our native land. To catch my brother and me up on our heritage, my parents took us to every museum, tumbledown castle, and cathedral we passed, so I was exposed to literally dozens of Europe's most beautiful Romanesque, Gothic, baroque, and rococo churches. Even though we attended no services, I still recall vividly nearly three decades later the sense of awe and reverence those temples of soaring stone and light inspired in me. Our age has lost the secret of raising the soul's eye to God through sacred architecture, but across the centuries those medieval masons gave me my first glimpse of the Spirit that animates all of creation.

On my eleventh birthday, my father was transferred to the West German consulate general in Atlanta, Georgia, where I was introduced to American culture via a hotel TV screen: *I Dream of Jeannie*, professional wrestling (Rick "the Nature Boy" Flair v. Chief Wahoo McDaniel), and the Reverend Ernest Angeley telling me to "Put your hand against that television screen and say 'Baaaaaaby Jesus.'" Somehow I managed to resist poor Ernest's attempts to evangelize me, nor was I persuaded by the soft-spoken young minister at the ruinously expensive Episcopal high school to which my parents sent me. Wednesdays there were "chapel day," which meant we had to wear ties and sit still for fifty minutes — perhaps the most effective means of paganizing children known to man. Certainly it worked on me, and when I began reading Buddhist books in my mid-teens, I even had a positive alternative to the weekly snooze-fest on "chapel day."

In those years I was spiritually hampered by an intellectual growth spurt that made it too easy to outshine my contemporaries. If I was *this* good all on my own, who needed God or religion? And how could anyone but the simple-minded believe that a Palestinian revolutionary walked on water and returned from the dead two millennia ago? I was too smart for all that.

But Buddhism met my high standards. Here I found sophisticated and plausible answers to philosophical questions like the problems of evil, without being asked to believe in childish miracle stories. Moreover, the Buddha had promised that *nirvana,* the release from *samsaric* existence, lay within our power if we applied ourselves. And, most intriguingly, my otherwise invincible intellect actually failed to crack Zen *koans,* or meditative riddles — so there really had to be something to all this Buddhism stuff, right?

Upon my graduation from high school, one of this country's top ten universities awarded me an academic scholarship that not only paid for my tuition but also covered rent, food, and even spending money. The Buddhist boy genius had come into his own, so it seemed. But less than two years later, on April 30, 1986, I was arrested for double murder and entered the belly of the beast: the court and prison system.

I will not bore you here with the details of my trial, appeals, and incarceration, since that story has been told elsewhere. The essential facts are these: when I was eighteen, I covered up the double murder of my then-girlfriend's parents and eventually was convicted of actually committing this crime. These events, as profoundly life-altering as they were, appeared to have no overt impact on my spiritual development, however. I continued to consider myself a Buddhist, though I had no contact with other believers and restricted the practice of my faith to a steady diet of books and occasional attempts at meditation.

It was not until the fall of 1994 that I reached my great turning point: a conversion to Christianity that was prompted by Pope John Paul II and NASA. That summer the pope forbade Catholics to watch the movie *The Last Temptation of Christ,* with predictable results in my case, at least. Since I could not go to a cinema, I quickly ordered the original novel by Nikos Kazantzakis — forbidden fruit tastes so much better! But in this book's pages I made an amazing and unexpected discovery: a (fictional) Jesus I not only liked, but empathized with and even admired. This was not the sappy wimp I remembered from "chapel day" but a complex human being who suffered and doubted and struggled with his destiny, much as I suffered and doubted and struggled with mine. Could the religion founded on his life and death hold some meaning for me after all?

I began to read the New Testament consciously and voluntarily for the first time in my life and, after an indecisive encounter with the Synoptics, fell in love with the Gospel according to John. One verse in particular touched the very center of my being and quite nearly brought me to tears: "Greater love has no one than this, that he lay down his life for his friends" (John 15:13). Like some supernaturally bright light, that sentence illumined a terrible night in my own life, changing its meaning though not the sad facts. I still choke up every time I read this passage.

What completed my conversion was the publication in a national magazine of those first, magnificent photographs from NASA's Hubble Space Telescope. While looking at the swirl of the galaxies around their mysterious, glowing centers, I had a kind of epiphany: both the physical force of gravity, which set those stars to circling, and the human emotion of love *were forms of attraction — or love!* Come to think of it, electrons could be said to love the nuclei they orbit, just as sunflowers love the sun they follow across the sky — yet more cases of attraction. Could this be what the New Testament meant when it claimed that "God is love," and that it is in this universal force that we "live and move and have our being" (1 John 4:16; Acts 17:28)? Did the Psalmist see what I saw when he wrote that "the heavens declare the glory of God" (Psalm 19:1)?

My tentative "yes" led me to contact the Reverend Beverly R. Cosby, one of whose parishioners visited me regularly at that time. Bev was the brother of the Reverend Gordon Cosby, founder of Washington, DC's Church of the Saviour, made famous by Elizabeth O'Connor's books. What attracted me to Bev was the radical commitment to "the inner and the outer way," which seemed to adhere closest to the model Christ gave us: full members of his congregation not only had to spend an hour each day in silent prayer, but also had to dedicate large amounts of time and money to serve society's outcasts. That combination of the spiritual and the practical produced their town's first interracial swimming pool and summer camp in the 1960s, low-cost housing for dozens of poor families, homeless and battered women's shelters, an AIDS hospice, and a dozen further ministries — all with only a handful of people.

Their leading texts, apart from the Bible, were Dietrich Bonhoeffer's *Life Together,* Henri Nouwen's works (he was a personal friend of Bev's), and Father Thomas Keating's books on Centering Prayer. It was with these works that I began my own education as a Christian, and for the next six years, I read voraciously: everything from Josephus to Bultmann. Absorbing the thoughts of great Christian writers became my primary means of practicing my new faith, along with twice daily Bible reading, verbal prayer, and monthly tithing of my prison wages to Feed the Children.

Apart from the Bible, the book that influenced me the most during this period was the *New St. Jerome Biblical Commentary,* which, to my mind, remains unsurpassed. It simply went deeper into the scriptural text than any of the other commentaries I bought, *and* it provided ancient and medieval exegetical views. These in particular came as a monumental surprise to me; until now, I had never encountered the thoughts of Jerome and Augustine and Aquinas, and thus I did not realize that they had developed a Christian philosophical edifice that was at least as sophisticated and satisfying as the Buddhists I had admired from my teens onward. And to think, the only reason I had bought the *New St. Jerome's* was because it was on sale!

So I continued my theological reading and twice-daily verbal prayers until, in the winter of 1999 and 2000, I came to an end. An end to *what,* I hardly know how to explain. All I can say is that the inner resources which had sustained me for fourteen years of incarceration (at that point) finally failed me. Perhaps it was nothing more than the cumulative weight of my miseries: having my arm broken twice by other inmates, spending three years under threat of execution, being nearly raped by another prisoner, hearing of my mother's death through alcoholism, and much else besides. Or perhaps God had finally brought me to a place where I had to let go of my self.

Learning to let go of the self — one's physical hungers, emotional desires, and intellectual preening — and opening oneself to God in silence is one way to describe Centering Prayer. Years earlier, Bev Cosby had sent me one of Father Thomas Keating's yellow leaflets on this spiritual discipline — basically, a reinvigoration of our age-old but nearly forgotten Christian tradition of contemplative prayer — and now, at this severe crisis point in my life, that yellow leaflet somehow fluttered out of my accumulated papers and into my hands.

I remembered how Bev occasionally mentioned that it was Centering Prayer, and Centering Prayer alone, that gave him the astonishingly deep, still energy he spent so recklessly on the helpless and homeless, the drunk and despairing. If this was really the secret of my mentor's beautiful spirit, perhaps it was time for me to give it a try, too. My intellect alone could not lift me out of the spiritual hole in which I found myself. That much was clear.

And so I embarked on a marvelous journey that continues to this day: I learned a new way of relating to God and the world that uses no words and no grasping with the mind, but relies on a fragile inner silence through which the Spirit enters me and I enter it. This journey has been tough at times — Centering Prayer is definitely not for the impatient — but it quickly began to transform my life. When I was shot with a rubber bullet a few months after beginning to practice this discipline — the guard had been aiming at another inmate — my first response was to sit down for some contemplation, and it was contemplation that eventually helped me find seeds of grace even in this traumatic experience.

In January of 2001, roughly one year after I began to practice Centering Prayer, the U.S. Supreme Court denied my attorney's final appeal petition without even granting a hearing. This came as a complete shock to me, because I *knew* I was no more guilty of double murder than Joseph was of raping Potiphar's wife. Over the previous fifteen years (at that time), I had held despair at bay with the firm belief that "the greatest legal system on earth" would *eventually* give me justice, clear my name, and return me to Germany. But that hope, that crutch was now gone.

My response to this living death sentence (life in prison without realistic hope of being granted parole) was, I believe, a gift of grace from God: I began to write a book entitled *The Way of the Prisoner: Breaking the Chains of Self through Centering Prayer and Centering Practice.* Its premise is that all of us are imprisoned in one way or another, whether by illness or an emotional trauma or a "real" jail. And the truth is that some of us will never leave our prisons. Sometimes, our crosses really do end in death.

Yet we can still experience genuine liberation as we struggle toward our own personal Golgotha — by freeing ourselves of our self, that urgent voice within that cries, "me, me, me," and complains so bitterly of its unjust fate. "The more completely a man renounces worldly things, the more perfectly he dies to self by conquest of the self, the sooner will grace be given, . . . and the nearer to God will it raise the heart set free from the world," wrote Thomas à Kempis in *The Imitation of Christ.*[1] And the wonderful thing is that this truth need not remain at the level of pious sentiment but can be turned into practical reality through a spiritual discipline that even a dumb convict like me managed to learn: Centering Prayer, or contemplation.

What Centering Prayer taught me, and can teach anyone who practices it, is that our prisons can become instruments of grace. Father Thomas Merton, the great contemplative author whose path *nearly* crossed mine in the year after my birth in Bangkok, Thailand, once wrote in a poem,

> Life is this simple.
> We are living in a world that is absolutely transparent,
>   and God is shining through it all the time. . . .
> God shows Godself everywhere,
>   in everything,
>   in people and in things and in nature and in events[2]

—and even in our suffering, our chains. Christ himself knew this well: it was only on the cross that he could show us what divine, self-giving, self-emptying love looked like in practice.

Another thing Centering Prayer taught me was how to come to terms with the crime that had sent me to prison. To some extent, this part of my inner journey is less important, since whatever peace I have found is of no relevance to the two murder victims, their relatives, or even my own family. My then-girlfriend's parents remain dead, and many innocent bystanders remain grief-stricken. Why should anyone care that I, the man convicted of this double homicide, have developed a new perspective on my role in this tragedy?

Certainly no one should care because of *me*. But the fact that I can write those words is in itself of some interest, I would argue, since the plain truth is that I did not murder my girlfriend's parents, and I have spent more than half of my life in prison for a crime I did not commit.

During the first decade and a half of my incarceration, this horrific injustice was the focal point of my existence, the only thing that mattered to me. But Centering Prayer showed me another way of living my life, a different focal point: Jesus. And even if you do not care about *me,* you might still care to hear this part of my story in case you or someone you love is struggling with a fate as cruel and unjust as is mine. There *is* hope.

I reached that hope through Centering Prayer. In *The Dialogue,* Catherine of Siena described this spiritual discipline as being "locked up in the house of self-knowledge" — an irresistible turn of phrase for a prisoner like myself, as one can imagine.[3] Locked up in my own house of self-knowledge in the penitentiary, I learned to face my sin and guilt, fear and pain, regret and shame while Centering. All these, I came to see, were facets of the self that came between me and the Spirit that animates the universe.

Our spiritual forefathers and foremothers, like Catherine of Siena, understood much better than we do today how important a lively and continual awareness of sinfulness is for sustained inner renewal. To us, their writings seem almost masochistically preoccupied with the sordid details of their transgressions. But I believe this is the very foundation of their spiritual greatness. Real saints never allow themselves to forget that even their best-intentioned acts carry within them some secret taint of selfishness or pride: "There is no one just, not even one" (Romans 3:10). Once this insight penetrates deeply in prayer, casting aside the self becomes a joyful act of liberation, and God can finally take over.

As far as the double murder in which I was involved is concerned, I came to see in prayer that guilt and innocence are much more complicated than I had thought at first. The truth is that I have much to be repentant for, and my incarceration is not totally unjust.

I could have prevented the killing of my girlfriend's parents if I had been less cowardly, more loving, more willing to help the person who committed the crime before it was too late. I failed to be my brother's keeper. And I knew this as soon as the real killer confessed the murders to me. My own moral culpability in failing to prevent the crime was, in fact, one of the primary reasons why I agreed to cover it up.

That meant lying — to my parents, to my friends, to the police, and ultimately to myself. With those lies, I hurt the victims' family, my own family, myself, and probably even the actual murderer. The harm my lies caused reached its terrible climax when my mother drank herself to death eleven years after my arrest. It took that long for her broken heart to kill her.

Since my mother's passing in 1997, my two life sentences have actually been easier to bear: one of them I now feel I deserve. But the story of my faith journey, my pilgrim's progress, does not end there. What happened after I accepted my sin and guilt was that God granted me the grace of conversion and renewal. What happened is . . . Easter.

When I began to write *The Way of the Prisoner* in January 2001, in response to the Supreme Court's denial of my lawyer's appeal, I did not expect that my work would ever be published. The only books by prisoners that seemed to make it into print were tell-all, "true crime" accounts of particularly notorious trials. What publisher would even bother to look at my manuscript, an unlikely combination of Centering Prayer instruction, history of contemplative literature, spiritual autobiography, and prison diary?

Simply finishing the book proved to be nearly impossible. In the twelve months it took me to complete the first draft, the devil fought me as hard as he could: halfway through the book, I lost my father, and just after I finished it, Bev Cosby died too. But even in those very dark days, God's grace was working powerfully to build a new family for me.

Thanks to the mother of a fellow prisoner — Ann, the persistent widow of chapter 7 — photocopies of my book manuscript flooded out into the world and won me many new friends — including some highly committed and deeply spiritual Episcopalians, the kind of people my school chaplain should have brought in as guest speakers on "chapel day." One copy of *The Way of the Prisoner* even made it into the hands of Father Thomas Keating, the co-founder of the Centering Prayer movement, who was kind enough to pass it on to his own publisher. And after much cutting and rewriting, Gene Gollogly and Lantern Books finally brought my book to market in the fall of 2003.

The Way of the Prisoner is not breaking any sales records, of course, but it *is* changing the lives of some readers and a few inmates. At the Servant Leadership School in Washington, DC, a course on Centering Prayer has used my book as the sole instructional text for three semesters in a row. And in North Carolina, one reader has now become an assistant chaplain at a major city jail, bringing Jesus to the women inmates there.

All this would be miracle enough for one lifetime — but God did not stop there. In the fall of 2004, Lantern released my second book, *An Expensive Way to Make Bad People Worse: An Essay on Prison Reform from an Insider's Perspective,* and the John Jay College of Criminal Justice is now using it as assigned reading for an introduction to criminology course. The book you are holding now, *The Convict Christ: What the Gospel Says about Criminal*

Justice, is my third, and as I write these lines, a fourth is underway. Miracles *are* possible; they have happened to me.

None of this goes to my credit, of course; it is all God's doing, not mine. In fact, what Centering Prayer did and does is to get *me* out of the way so God has more room to use me. "He must increase, I must decrease," John the Baptist said in a context not too different from this one (John 3:30).

For me, the key to it all is more Centering Prayer, more time "locked up in the house of self-knowledge." I now practice Centering Prayer four times a day, roughly half an hour per session. By returning so often to my own brokenness, weakness, and failure in prayer, I learn to keep my eyes trained on Jesus, whose grace I need so desperately.

But I am not the only prisoner who needs Christ. There are 2.2 million other inmates in this country today, all of whom are in need of a Bev Cosby, to befriend them and teach them how to pray; a Thomas Keating, to open a crucial door for them; and a Gene Gollogly, to give them work, an opportunity to use their talents. All three of these men — especially Bev — were the face of Jesus for me; through them, the prisoner Jens could partake of the same new life of which the convict Christ was the first fruits (1 Corinthians 15:20, 23).

And through *you,* some inmate whose name you do not even know yet can also share in that resurrection, that Easter. *You* can become the face of Jesus, just like Bev.

Questions for Reflection and Discussion

1. Is it appropriate for the author to present details of his life behind bars in this book? On the one hand, Paul did not hesitate to make use of his own incarceration in his epistles: "my situation has turned out rather to advance the gospel, so that my imprisonment has become well known in Christ throughout the whole praetorium and to all the rest" (Philippians 1:12–13; see also Colossians 4:3; Ephesians 6:19–20). On the other

hand, Paul was guilty of no crime, whereas the author of this book is guilty at the very least of covering up a double murder. Is the author a trustworthy witness to the power of Christ *despite* the author's evil past — or perhaps *because* of it?

2. In many states, versions of so-called "Son of Sam" laws are used to attempt to confiscate royalties from books written by prison inmates. Because the original "Son of Sam" statute was overturned by the U.S. Supreme Court in 1991, such attempts usually — but not always — fail.[4] Do you think "Son of Sam" laws and royalty confiscations have the effect of discouraging both publishers and inmate-authors from bringing books like this one to market? What is more important from a public policy point of view: to encourage prison writers as a way to educate the public about correctional issues, or to punish convicted felons by confiscating their royalties?

3. In his Second Letter to Timothy, written from his Roman jail, Paul asks his friend to "bring the cloak I left with Carpus in Troas, the papyrus rolls and especially the parchments" (4:13). This suggests that prison ministry ought not to be restricted to preaching but should also include practical assistance: clothing, educational material, and perhaps also food and medical care. Now imagine yourself visiting an inmate and having him or her ask you for money to buy scented soap. Would that strike you as an unnecessary luxury, without spiritual or religious value? Or could it be that, in a world of unmitigated ugliness and squalor, even a simple bar of scented soap is a symbol of hope, a reminder that one is still a human being?

Conclusion

✠ ✠ ✠

I N THIS BOOK'S introduction, I argued that our Messiah did not
die a convict's death by accident, but that he chose to let himself
be executed as a criminal with the specific intent of revealing the
root of all evil: the refusal to acknowledge that even your worst
enemy is a child of God. When we lock someone in a cell, or hang
or electrocute or crucify him, this refusal takes on a social dimension
and thus seems to us to be justified. But on Golgotha Christ showed
us who is behind that locked door, whose neck is in the noose, who
sits in the chair, who hangs from the crossbeam: another son or
daughter of our common Abba.

Of course even some children of God occasionally need to be
confined for a time: to protect society, to make them confront the
evil they did, to maintain public respect for the community's rules,
perhaps even to save them from themselves. As someone who has
spent more than two decades behind bars, I know far better than
you ever will just how necessary prisons are for some folks! But
the ultimate hope and purpose of confinement must always be to
reform, to bring all those prodigal sons and daughters back to their
families — and to *our* family.

Some friends of mine tell me that America is not ready to hear
this message of our Lord's, and perhaps they are right. But it is
worth noting that the early church apparently paid close heed to
this theme of Jesus' teaching, and put it into practice.

When Paul and Silas were thrown into jail in Philippi, for instance, they could have done their time quietly and hoped for early
release through good behavior. Instead, they engaged in prison ministry, "praying and singing hymns to God, and the other prisoners

were listening to them" (Acts 16:25). So successful was this impromptu rehabilitative program that none of the convicts fled when
"all the prison doors flew open [due to] an earthquake.... 'Don't
harm yourself! We are all here,'" Paul shouted to the jailer, who
"was about to kill himself because he thought the prisoners had
escaped" (Acts 16:26, 28, 27).

Clearly, Paul and Silas had heard about the Gerasene demoniac,
the woman caught in adultery, the spirit of F. Lee Bailey and the
good thief. To them, these were not just nice, heartwarming stories,
but examples to follow. Reforming criminals is what Christ did, and
therefore what real Christians must also do.

So, are *you* a real Christian?

Notes

1. *The Sermon in the Synagogue at Nazareth*

1. Roy Walmsley, *World Prison Population List*, 3rd ed. (London: Home Office Research, Development and Statistics Directorate, 2002), 4–5; calculation based on an estimated U.S. population of 289,948,581 and a world population of 6,265,656,384.

2. Marc Mauer, *Race to Incarcerate* (New York: New Press, 1999), 82–84; Richard Willing, "Inmate Population Rises as Crime Drops," *USA Today*, July 28, 2003; Connie Cass, "Prison Population Grows by 2.9 Percent in 2003," Associated Press, May 28, 2004.

3. Marc Mauer, "Americans behind Bars: The International Use of Incarceration, 1992–1993," cited in Peter Wagner, *The Prison Index* (Springfield, MA: Prison Policy Initiative, 2003), 41; figure of 4,834 provided by Peter Wagner to author via personal correspondence, November 9, 2004, based on Bureau of Justice Statistics reports for 2003 (published in 2004).

4. See, as examples, the correctional departments of New York and Virginia: the NYDOCS is ranked #1 in "general fund, state operations" spending; SUNY is a bigger agency, but only because it also receives federal offset funds; source: New York State Division of the Budget, personal communication to Sarah J. Gallogly, September 17, 2003; Frank Green, "Prison Chief Defends Tenure," *Richmond Times-Dispatch*, September 16, 2002, B1; Fox Butterfield, "With Longer Sentences, Cost of Fighting Crime Is Higher," *New York Times*, May 3, 2004.

5. Richard Willing, "Crime Rate Hits 30-Year Low," *USA Today*, August 25, 2003.

6. Public Education Speaker Kit, Module 5, "Incarceration," Correctional Service of Canada, *www.csc-scc.gc/ca*.

7. Walmsley, *World Prison Population List*, 1; Cass, "Prison"; Pat Mayhew and Jan J. M. Van Dijk, *Criminal Victimisation in Eleven Industrialized Countries* (The Netherlands: Ministry of Justice, 1997); J. Van Kesteren, P. Mayhew, P. Niewbeerta, *Criminal Victimisation in Seventeen Industrialized Countries: Key Findings from the 2000 International Crime Victims Survey, 2000*, cited in Wagner, *Index*, 40.

8. Crime victimization" here refers not to incidents reported to police but to responses made to a household survey. See Wagner, *Index,* 40.

9. Caroline Schmidt, "Schwitzen statt sitzen," *Der Spiegel,* no. 30 (2003): 46.

10. Marc Mauer and Meda Chesney-Lind, eds., *Invisible Punishment: The Collateral Consequences of Mass Imprisonment* (New York: New Press, 2003), 280.

11. Paige M. Harrison and Allen J. Beck, *Prisoners in 2003* (Washington, DC: Bureau of Justice Statistics, 2004).

2. The Gerasene Demoniac

1. Etienne Benson, "Rehabilitate or Punish?" *Monitor on Psychology* (American Psychological Association) 34, no. 7 (July–August 2003): 47.

2. "The Health Status of Soon-to-Be-Released Inmates: A Report to Congress" (Washington, DC: National Commission on Correctional Care, November–December 2002), xii.

3. Fox Butterfield, "Study Finds Hundreds of Thousands of Inmates Mentally Ill," *New York Times,* October 22, 2003.

4. Benson, "Rehabilitate."

5. Butterfield, "Study."

6. Paul von Zielbauer, "Report on State Prisons Cites Inmates' Mental Illness," *New York Times,* October 22, 2003.

7. Nicholas M. Horrock, "Hundreds of Thousands Raped in U.S. Lockups," United Press International, July 31, 2002.

8. *HIV in Prisons* (Washington, DC: Bureau of Justice Statistics, 2000), 2; Centers for Disease Control, "Morbidity and Mortality Weekly Report," February 26, 2003, vol. 52.

9. The Bureau of Justice Statistics found that 141,000 women were raped in the United States in 1999; according to the FBI, 89,107 of these rapes were reported to police. Fred Dickey, "Rape, How Funny Is It?" *Los Angeles Times Magazine,* November 3, 2002, 22; Eli Lehrer, "Hell behind Bars," *National Review,* February 5, 2001.

3. The Woman Caught in Adultery

1. See also Deuteronomy 17:12, 13:5–11, 17:7, 19:9, 21:21, 22:21–22, 24, 24:7; Judges 20:13; 2 Samuel 19:3.

2. See also Leviticus 20:2, 24:14, 23; Deuteronomy 13:10, 17:5, 7, 21:19, 21:21; Joshua 7:25; 1 Kings 21:10, 13, 12:18; 2 Chronicles 10:18.

3. J. Greenberg, "Crime and Punishments," *The Interpreter's Dictionary of the Bible* (New York: Abingdon Press, 1962), 1:736 (emphasis added).

4. Christopher D. Marshall, *Beyond Retribution: A New Testament Vision for Justice, Crime and Punishment* (Grand Rapids: W. B. Eerdmans, 2001), 212–13.

5. See for example: W. C. Bailey, "Deterrence and the Death Penalty for Murders in Utah: A Time Analysis," *Journal of Contemporary Law* 5, no. 1 (1978); "An Analysis of the Deterrent Effect of the Death Penalty for Murders in California," *Southern California Law Review* 52, no. 3 (1979); B. E. Forst, "The Deterrent Effect of Capital Punishment: A Cross-State Analysis of the 1960s," *Minnesota Law Review* 61 (1977); S. H. Decker and C. W. Kohfeld, "Capital Punishment and Executions in the Lone Star State: A Deterrence Study," *Criminal Justice Research Bulletin* (Criminal Justice Center, Sam Houston State University) 3, no. 12 (1988).

4. John the Baptist's Defender

1. Mark Holmberg, "The Other Side of the Story," *Richmond Times-Dispatch,* January 25, 2004.

2. Bill Geroux, "Judge Isn't Sure Giarratano Evidence Exists," *Richmond Times-Dispatch,* January 22, 2004.

3. Colman McCarthy, "Peace within the Walls," *www.truthinaction.net/Allactivists/JoeGiarratano/articles/peacewithinwalls.htm.*

4. Colman McCarthy, "Prisoner's Life Is Radically Different from Time of His '79 Conviction," *Virginian Pilot,* February 26, 2004.

5. Peg Tyre, "Reversing the Verdict," *Newsweek,* December 16, 2002.

6. Adam Liptak, "Study Suspects Thousands of False Convictions," *New York Times,* May 4, 2004.

7. Richard Willing, "Justice Dept.: DNA Tests for Guilty Jam System," *USA Today,* May 13, 2004.

8. Leonard Pitts, "In Coleman Case, Virginia Fears Finding Out the Truth," *Richmond Times-Dispatch,* May 17, 2004.

9. "Ex-FBI Biologist Enters Guilty Plea," Associated Press, May 19, 2004.

10. Deborah Hastings, "Memo Cites Evidence of Alleged Misconduct," Associated Press, April 21, 2004.

11. John Solomon, "FBI Lab DNA Probe Expands," Associated Press, April 28, 2003.

12. "State Pursues Leak, Not Lead, in Murder Case," *Virginian Pilot,* May 9, 2004.

5. *John the Baptist's Execution*

1. Allen Beck and Bernard Shipley, *Recidivism of Prisoners Released in 1983* (Washington, DC: Bureau of Justice Statistics, April 1989).

2. Michael Hardy, "ACLU: Prison Care Lacking," *Richmond Times-Dispatch,* May 8, 2003, A1.

3. *Accountable to No One — The Virginia Department of Corrections and Prisoner Medical Care* (Washington, DC: ACLU, 2003), 7.

4. "The Dark Side of America," *New York Times,* May 17, 2004.

5. Response to author's "Informal Mechanism" by Brunswick Correctional Center Medical Department staff member, October 27, 2003.

6. *Accountable to No One,* 3, 16.

7. "Dark Side."

8. Hardy, "ACLU: Prison Care Lacking."

9. Ibid.

6. *The Good Samaritan*

1. Eli Lehrer, "Hell behind Bars," *National Review,* February 5, 2001.

2. Adam Liptak, "Alabama Prison at Center of Suit over AIDS Policy," *New York Times,* October 26, 2003.

3. Neely Tucker, "Study Warns of Rising Tide of Released Inmates," *Washington Post,* May 21, 2003, A1.

4. Patrick A. Langan and David J. Levin, *Recidivism of Prisoners Released in 1994* (Washington, DC: Bureau of Justice Statistics, June 2002).

5. John J. DiIulio Jr., "Two Million Prisoners Are Enough," *Wall Street Journal,* March 12, 1999.

6. Cal Thomas, "Three Strikes and You're Broke," *Richmond Times-Dispatch,* November 17, 2003.

7. *Profile of State Prisoners under Age 18, 1985–1997* (Washington, DC: Bureau of Justice Statistics, January 2002), 1, 2.

8. Frank Green, "Prison-Rape Issue Gets Closer Look," *Richmond Times-Dispatch,* July 10, 2003.

9. Associated Press, "Senate Panel Stops Prison-Rape Bill," *Newport News Daily Press,* January 27, 2004, C3.

10. Michael M. Horrock, "Hundreds of Thousands Raped in U.S. Lock-Ups," United Press International, July 31, 2002.

11. *Ruiz v. Estelle,* 503 F.Supp. 1265 (S.D.Tex. 1980), aff'd in part and vacated in part, 679 F.2d 1115 (5th Cir.), amended in part, 688 F.2d 266 (5th Cir. 1982), cert. denied 460 U.S. 1042 (1983).

12. Green, "Prison-Rape Issue."

13. Eli Lehrer, "A Blind Eye, Still Turned," *National Review,* June 2, 2003.

14. Linda Greenhouse, "Justices Agree to Evaluate Prison Policy Based on Race," *New York Times,* March 2, 2004; *Johnson v. Gomez,* No. 03-636.

15. *Cunningham v. Sandahl,* 1998 WL 157415 (N.D.Ill.).

16. Associated Press, "Senate Panel."

17. Horrock, "Hundreds of Thousands."

7. The Persistent Widow and the Unjust Judge

1. Walter Wink, *The Powers That Be* (New York: Galilee/Random House, 1998), 103–4.

2. CBS Evening News, August 10, 2003.

3. Marc Mauer, *Race to Incarcerate* (New York: New Press, 1999), 82–84; Richard Willing, "Inmate Population Rises as Crime Drops," *USA Today,* July 28, 2003; Connie Cass, "Prison Population Grows by 2.9 percent in 2003," Associated Press, May 28, 2004; Richard Willing, "More Adults Have Prison Experience," *USA Today,* August 18, 2003, 3A; Neely Tucker, "Study Warns of Rising Tide of Released Inmates," *Washington Post,* May 21, 2003, A1; Paige M. Harrison and Allen J. Beck, *Prisoners in 2003* (Washington, DC: Bureau of Justice Statistics, 2004).

4. Henry Ruth and Keith R. Reitz, *The Challenge of Crime: Rethinking Our Response* (Cambridge, MA: Harvard University Press, 2003), 95–96.

5. "Can Parole Cut Crime?" *Parade,* December 10, 2003, 17.

6. Stefanie Pfeiffer, "One Strike Against the Elderly: Growing Old in Prison," *Medill News Service,* August 2002; U.S. Census Bureau, quoted in Joshua Maher, "The Quality of Care of Elderly Inmates in Prison," KELN.org May 2000. Penologists define "elderly" as fifty-five and over for convicts; prisoners' physical age is generally ten years higher than their chronological age due to poor health.

7. Jim Krane, "The Graying of America's Prisons: An Emerging Corrections Crisis," *APB News,* April 12, 1999; Matthew Nehmer, "GW Professor Jonathan Turley to Testify," GW News Center, George Washington University, February 24, 2003.

8. Joanne Kimberlin, "Victim's Vigil," *Virginian Pilot,* April 5, 2004, A1.

9. Frank Green, "Parole Policy Unused," *Richmond Times-Dispatch,* September 14, 2003, B1.

10. Wink, *The Powers That Be,* 181.

8. The Judgment of the Nations

1. Paul Martin Andrews, Letter to the Editor, *Washington City Paper,* September 17, 2004.

2. Stephanie Stoughton, "Convicted Molester Found Dead in Prison," *Associated Press,* January 14, 2004.

3. Frank Green and Bill Geroux, "Ausley's Death in Prison Probed," *Richmond Times-Dispatch,* January 15, 2004, A1.

4. See *www.jenssoering.com/trial.*

5. Frank Schmalleger, *Criminology Today: An Integrative Introduction,* 2nd ed. (Upper Saddle River, NJ: Prentice-Hall, 1999), 27; Caroline W. Harlow, "Prior Abuse Reported by Inmates and Probationers," Bureau of Justice Selected Findings (Washington, DC: U.S. Department of Justice, 1999).

6. Green and Geroux, "Ausley's Death."

7. *Probation and Parole Violators in State Prisons, 1991* (Washington, DC: Bureau of Justice Statistics, August 1995).

8. Karen Kersting, "New Hope for Sex Offender Treatment," *Monitor on Psychology* (American Psychological Association) 34, no. 7 (July–August 2003): 52–53, citing R. Karl Hanson's study in *Sex Abuse: A Journal of Research and Treatment* 14, no. 2 (2002).

9. Interview with SORT staff member who asked to remain anonymous, conducted by author on October 29, 2003.

10. Andrews, Letter to the Editor, September 17, 2004.

11. Associated Press, "State Unveils High-Tech Center for Sexually Violent Predators," *Virginian Pilot,* September 17, 2003, B12.

12. Andrews, Letter to the Editor, September 17, 2004.

13. Carolyn Marshall, "Taking the Laws into Their Own Hands," *New York Times,* April 20, 2004.

14. Juan Antonio Lizama, "Predators Get Amenities," *Richmond Times-Dispatch,* September 17, 2003.

15. Green and Geroux, "Ausley's Death."

16. Amy Jeter and Louis Hansen, "Child Rapist, Kidnapper Found Slain in Prison Cell," *Virginian Pilot,* January 15, 2004.

17. Ibid.

18. Frank Green, "Prison Violence Report Removed," *Richmond Times-Dispatch,* June 27, 2003.

19. Frank Green, "Cellmate Charged in Killing of Ausley," *Richmond Times-Dispatch,* June 4, 2004.

20. Ibid.

21. Frank Green, "Inmate Resisted Cell with Ausley," *Richmond Times-Dispatch,* June 18, 2004.

22. Green, "Cellmate Charged."

23. Frank Green, "Inmate Resisted."

24. Frank Green, "Ausley Case under Review," *Richmond Times-Dispatch,* June 30, 2004.

25. Associated Press, "Report: Priest Was Placed in Wrong Unit," *Richmond Times-Dispatch*, February 4, 2004.

26. Associated Press, "Sex Offenders: State Seeks Funds for Facility in Nottoway County," *Virginian Pilot*, January 16, 2004.

27. Kathryn Orth, "Nottoway Views Mixed on Sex-Offender Facility," *Richmond Times-Dispatch*, February 20, 2004.

28. Jens Soering, *The Way of the Prisoner — Breaking the Chains of Self through Centering Prayer and Centering Practice* (New York: Lantern Books, 2003), 291.

9. The Paraclete

1. Richard C. Goemann, "System Strives toward Equal Justice," *Richmond Times-Dispatch*, January 1, 2004.

2. "A Small Step Forward," *New York Times*, March 22, 2004.

3. "Va. Defense for Poor Is Lacking, Report Says," *Virginian Pilot*, November 20, 2003.

4. Deborah Smith Bailey, "Alternatives to Incarceration," *Monitor on Psychology* (American Psychological Association) 34, no. 7 (July–August 2003): 56, 55.

5. Peter Anderson, "Treatment with Teeth," *American Prospect* (December 2003): 46.

6. Bailey, "Alternatives to Incarceration," and Anderson, "Treatment with Teeth."

7. J. Consedine, *Restorative Justice — Healing the Effects of Crime* (Lyttleton, N.Z.: Ploughshares, 1995), 81–97.

8. Lawrence W. Sherman and Heather Strang, *The Right Kind of Shame for Crime Prevention*, RISE Working Papers, no. 1 (Canberra: Australian National University, 1997), online at *www.aic.gov.au/rjustice/rise/working/ risepap1.html*; Heather Strang and Lawrence W. Sherman, *The Victim's Perspective*, RISE Working Papers, no. 2 (1997), online at *http://eprints .anu.edu.au/archive/00001100/00/risepap2.html*; Lawrence W. Sherman and Geoffrey C. Barnes, *Restorative Justice and Offenders' Respect for the Law*, RISE Working Papers, no. 3 (1997), online at *http://eprints.anu.edu .au/archive/00001101/00/risepap3.html*; Sherman and Strang, *Restorative Justice and Deterring Crime*, RISE Working Papers, no. 4 (1997), online at *http://eprints.anu.edu.au/archive/00001102/00/risepap4.html.*

9. *Breaking the Rules* (Washington, DC: Center for Public Integrity, 2003), see *www. publicintegrity.org.*

10. The Legionnaires in the Praetorium

1. Rick Hampson, "Abuse Less Shocking in Light of History," *USA Today*, May 13, 2004.

2. Rex Bowman, "Charges Out of Character?" *Richmond Times-Dispatch*, May 1, 2004.

3. Dennis Cauchon, "Former Guard Has a History of Complaints," *USA Today*, May 17, 2004.

4. "Improvement to U.S. Prisons Sought," Associated Press, May 16, 2004.

5. Frank Green, "Former Va. Prison Director Speaks about Abuses in Iraq," *Richmond Times-Dispatch*, May 20, 2004.

6. Fox Butterfield, "Treatment of Prisoners Is Called Routine," *New York Times*, May 8, 2004.

7. Ibid.

8. Laurence Hammack, "Connecticut Settles Lawsuits in Supermax Deaths," *Roanoke Times*, March 15, 2002.

9. John Diamond, "Early Signs Were Given Secondary Priority," *USA Today*, May 10, 2004.

10. Alan Levin, "Pa. Hometown Proud of MP Who Blew Whistle on Scandal," *USA Today*, May 10, 2004.

11. Hampson, "Abuse Less Shocking."

12. Anahad O'Connor, "Pressure to Go Along with Abuse Is Strong," *New York Times*, May 14, 2004.

13. James Q. Whitman, "Prisoner Degradation Abroad — and At Home," *Washington Post*, May 10, 2004.

11. Simon of Cyrene

1. Neely Tucker, "Study Warns of Rising Tide of Released Inmates," *Washington Post*, May 21, 2003, p. A1.

2. Eric Lottke, "Hobbling a Generation" (Baltimore: National Center on Institutions and Alternatives, 1997); see also *Washington Post*, August 26, 1997, B1.

3. Marc Mauer, "The Sentencing Project," quoted in Jens Soering, *An Expensive Way to Make Bad People Worse: An Essay on Prison Reform from an Insider's Perspective* (New York: Lantern Books, 2004), Conclusion.

4. *Federal Register*, February 23, 2004 (vol. 62, no. 35), FR DOC 04-3844, p. 8202.

5. Census 2000, Table QT-P3, *census.gov*.

6. Laura Mansuerus, "Prison Union Seeks Ouster of the Chief of Corrections," *New York Times*, December 31, 2003.

7. Joanne Mariner, *No Escape: Male Rape in U.S. Prisons* (New York: Human Rights Watch, 2001).

8. Adam Liptak, "Study Revises Texas' Standing as a Death Penalty Leader," *New York Times,* February 14, 2004, citing J. Blume, T. Eisenberg, and M. T. Wells, "Explaining Death Row's Population and Racial Composition" (Cornell Law School and the Death Penalty Information Center, 2004).

12. The Good Thief

1. Warren St. John, "Professors with a Past," *New York Times,* August 9, 2003, A13.

2. Tara Jen Ambrosio and Vincent Schiraldi, *From Classrooms to Cellblocks: A National Perspective* (Washington, DC: Justice Policy Institute, 1999).

3. *Cellblocks or Classrooms?* (Washington, DC: Justice Policy Institute, 2002).

4. Calculation based on Table 6.38, *Sourcebook of Criminal Justice Statistics 2000* (Washington, DC: Bureau of Justice Statistics, 2000); "Education as Crime Prevention," OSI Criminal Justice Initiative, September 1997.

5. "Education and Correctional Populations" (Washington, DC: Bureau of Criminal Justice Statistics, January 2003), Table 4.

6. *www.changingminds.ws/brochure/* viewed January 3, 2003.

7. Ibid.

8. New York Department of Correctional Services, "Follow-Up Study of a Sample of Offenders Who Earned High School Equivalency Diplomas (G.E.D.s) While Incarcerated in D.O.C.S," May 2001, Figure 1.

9. New York Department of Correctional Services, "Analysis of Return Dates of the Inmate College Program Participants," August 1991.

10. Neely Tucker, "Study Warns of Rising Tide of Released Inmates," *Washington Post,* May 21, 2003, A1.

11. Patrick A. Langan and David J. Levin, *Recidivism of Prisoners Released in 1994* (Washington, DC: Bureau of Justice Statistics, June 2002).

12. "A Catch-22 for Ex-Offenders," *New York Times,* April 6, 2004.

13. The Bad Thief

1. Donna Leinwand, "Study Cites Sentencing Laws for Rise in Prison Life Terms," *New York Times,* May 12, 2004.

14. The Resurrection

1. Thomas à Kempis, *The Imitation of Christ,* IV, 15, trans. L. Sherley-Price (New York: Penguin Books, 1952).

2. Quoted without attribution in Esther de Waal, "Attentiveness," *Weavings — A Journal of the Christian Spiritual Life* 16, no. 4 (July–August 2002).

3. St. Catherine of Siena, *The Dialogue,* trans. S. Noffke (New York and Mahwah, NJ: Paulist Press, 1980), 120.

4. *Simon & Schuster v. State Crime Victims Board,* 502 U.S. 105 (1991); see also *Keenan v. Superior Court,* 02 S.O.S. 925 (2002), and *Opinion of the Justices to the Senate of the Commonwealth of Massachusetts,* 264 N.E.2d 343 (2002); contrast Bob Minzesheimer, "The Written Word Unshackled," *USA Today,* April 20, 2004; see also *www.jenssoering.com,* FAQs.

About the Author

A citizen of Germany, Jens Soering was a nineteen-year-old honors student at the University of Virginia when he was arrested in 1986 for the murders of his girlfriend's parents. Fictionalized accounts of his case have been featured on CourtTV, A&E, Discovery Channel, and National Geographic TV. For newspaper articles about his trial and appeal, see *www.jenssoering.com*.

Jens began practicing Centering Prayer in 2000 while housed at a supermax prison and converted to Catholicism in 2002. In 2003, Lantern Books published his first book, *The Way of the Prisoner: Breaking the Chains of Self through Centering Prayer and Centering Practice*, which has been well reviewed in the *National Catholic Reporter*. His second book, *An Expensive Way to Make Bad People Worse: An Essay on Prison Reform from an Insider's Perspective*, was published by Lantern Books in 2004 and has been used by the John Jay College of Criminal Justice, New York, as assigned reading.

Jens cannot be contacted by e-mail, but his Web site lists his current postal address.

About the Cover Art and Artist

One Body: Covered by Grace is a 12′ x 17′ textile paint on muslin quilt, the result of sacred art workshops by the artist Lynne Marie at MCI-Framingham (Massachusetts), a maximum security women's prison. Lynne Marie conceived the idea for the quilt and, under her direction, each of 176 women inmates painted self-portraits on handkerchief-like squares of cloth. The pieces were then carefully joined together by the artist and eleven volunteers outside the prison, forming a unified body that reflects the image of Christ.

An accomplished outsider artist and an advocate of art in women's prisons, Lynne Marie has studios on the Williamsburg Waterfront in Brooklyn and on Nantucket Island. Her work in prison ministry grew over five years, producing and facilitating art programs to revive the creative spirit.

For more information about the *One Body: Covered by Grace* quilt and the artist, Lynne Marie, please visit *www.jubileeartist.com*.